SQUEAKY
GOURM

Published by Fish Lips Ink LLC. www.fishlipsink.com

Printed in China

Title: Squeaky Gourmet

ISBN 0-9795606-0-8

This book is not intended for use as a substitute for advice and consultation from a qualified medical professional. Before you begin any diet or exercise program, you should consult with your physician. All matters regarding diet and health require medical supervision. If you have any symptoms of illness or injury you should confer with your doctor immediately. Your health needs are your own; treatment needs to be geared to your specific needs based on your doctor's approval and suggestions. No book can replace the care of your doctor. You are encouraged to work closely with your doctor or dietician for optimum results in any wellness program. The authors and publishers shall not be liable or responsible for any injury, loss, damage occasioned to any person who acts or fails to act as a result of any information presented in this book, whether or not the loss, injury or damage is due in any way to any negligent act or omissions, breach of duty, or default on the authors or publishers part. The brand names in this book are not intended as product endorsement. Products included are not superior to like products not included in this book. Opinions expressed in this book are solely the opinions of the individual authors and are not those of the publishers.

Nutritional data collected and reported from each recipe was provided by Diet Power Software www.dietpower.com . The nutritional and other information from this book is not intended to be and does not constitute health care or medical advice and must not be used to make any diagnosis specific to a dietary need. Diet Power software is in no way affiliated with the authors or the publishers.

Text Was Written By Maureen Jeanson with Recipes created and compiled by Jamie Wilson

"I loved this Book! These dishes can be prepared for anyone not just someone on a fitness journey. I loved the holistic approach to food as well as the entertaining way Squeaky Gourmet was written. I plan to keep this book on stock at my college bookstore."

Dorene Peterson BA, Dip. NT, Dip. Acu-
President of Australasian College of Health Science
www.achs.edu

"This book is great for people just starting out on their fitness journey or for those die hards who are just looking for better recipes. **This book is GREAT!**"

John Sferes M.S. Cpt.,
Fitness Specialist Department of Defense
jsferes@yahoo.com

"The recipes were very simple and easy to prepare. No major fancy items needed for these recipes. Ya know, stuff we all have in our cupboards instead of last minute store runs for special ingredients of spices. As someone who is very health conscious and tracks all my macronutrients, I appreciated the nutritional breakdown to aid me in adding a recipe into meal plans and even tweaking it for hubby with his special nutritional needs."

Ileen Natic
Fitness/Physique Enthusiast and Mother of 5

"Maureen Jeanson is an excellent example of a true fitness educator, and every person who has the opportunity to work with her directly or read Squeaky Gourmet will truly benefit, physically and mentally. Her understanding of the demands of clients, busy schedules and most importantly the struggles of dealing with boring and monotonous foods makes her the perfect expert to teach us all how to prepare Simple… Clean… Foods. **I would make this a must have!**"

Patrick Gamboa B.S. MSS
Editor-in-Chief of ISSA Pro Trainer Online Magazine/
Editor-in-Chief of Associate Magazine
Vice President of Education
pgamboa@issaonline.com

Table of Contents

PROTEIN, *continued*

CARBOHYDRATES

FATS

Introduction

Maureen Jeanson C.M.H.

This is the portion of the book I have struggled with writing. About me, who I am and how I arrived here. I could tell you about my battle with fat which started long ago as a child. I could fill you in on the stories of childhood thoughts and ideals on what I was supposed to look like versus the young girl in the mirror. However, the more I think about those ideas, I realize that more people have struggled with those same thoughts than have not. So, who am I and what gives me the "authority" to write a book for you that will help you reach your own goals? I have found what works. I have had my own struggles and adversity and have succeeded where millions of people have not.

What now seems like a lifetime ago I became pregnant with my third son. The pregnancy was normal and I gained my normal pregnancy weight. The only difference was that I did not get to bring my son home with me. He passed away at birth and my husband and I were left with that intense grief and the battle to return to normal life. During that grief process my husband and I became very focused on bringing home a new child to our family. We never conceived again and seven months after our son died my husband was killed in an automobile accident. I am sharing this with you so you'll understand that I too have faced hardship and turmoil and I know how hard it is to accept the tragedy life can bestow on us when we are not looking. However, we can overcome tragedy and grow and learn from anything in life. Anything.

A few years after my husband's death I began dating again. The natural progression of our relationship led us to marriage and a new pregnancy. This pregnancy was where the largest portion of my weight crept on. My concern was for the baby and not my health at all. I ate anything to help the baby grow and to cover my fears of losing this child. Happily, my first daughter was born safely and healthy. I became pregnant again shortly after her birth and before I could lose even one pound of the weight I had just gained during that pregnancy. So there I was again, 9 months later with 2 little girls and about 80 pounds of happiness and fear displayed as fat rolls on my body.

When my second daughter was about 18 months old I decided along with two close friends that we no longer wanted to look like the mom in the minivan wearing the Winnie-the-Pooh shirt to tee ball games. I wanted to see a reflection of who I knew I was, not who I had become externally. I desired to be the sexy wife on my husband's arm, someone who looked normal and attractive. I felt dumpy and depressed, I lacked energy and vigor. Ok, truthfully I didn't even feel fun anymore. Not for my two young toddlers, my teenagers or for my husband. So, I decided to change.

I began with a clear eating plan. I mapped out clear goals and began my fitness journey. I used the encouragement of my friends and the determination of my Irish heritage to take the bull by the horns and succeed. You know what? I did it. I won. I reached my first goal in as little as four month's time. I lost 37 pounds and 38 inches off my body and felt brand new. Don't you want to feel brand new?

Please allow us to show you some simple recipes, some basic healthy ideas you can begin your own fitness journey. Don't set this book down and forget about it. Read the food tips, try out the recipes and make your plan.

It has been two years now since I began this fitness journey. I have lost 88 pounds of fat and completely reshaped my body. I am now a personal fitness trainer for the Navy I also run an online personal training business to help people just like you. I have a successful internet forum which I offer for free. I want people to feel the support and encouragement I felt from my friends. You can't do this alone, and I am here each step of the way to help you.

Don't waste another day.
Set your plan in action and begin Your Fitness Journey.
www.yourfitnessjourney.com

Jamie Wilson

I am still a work in progress as I am ultimately working toward good health. Tell you what, from where I started it has been a long road but I am getting closer to where I need to be on a daily basis. I have some medical issues that I'm still trying to work through but I am and the results are coming. I am a firm believer in the old ..." You are what you eat," so I am trying to eat only real, whole, unprocessed foods. If diseases such as cancer and diabetes can possibly be stopped by my eating real foods, exercising every day, and generally being good to my body, I'm giving it a try.

I am 40 years old, wife to an amazing man, and mother to a beautiful 4 year old daughter. I am also a Consulting Geologist in central Wyoming. I travel a lot and am often away from home for weeks at a time. I have learned how to take care of myself while traveling and how to make health a priority every day of my life.

Health. Mine was pretty good when I started this journey but it was getting worse each year. My family history is full of Diabetes and Cancer and I really didn't, and still don't, want to let myself slide in that direction due to poor eating and exercise habits.

I have been "playing" at getting in shape for at least 5 years. I would do great for a few months then completely crater. Then on to the next thing, another 3 months, then crater. In that time period I never followed any fad diets, I always ate 5 balanced meals a day, lifted weights and did cardio. It never stuck. I knew what to do but seemed to be missing something. I was soooo inconsistent.

I finally found the missing part, Moe. My trainer and now co-author Moe. Even though she was on the East Coast and I was in Wyoming, it clicked. She made sense. Her guidance was straightforward, no nonsense, and honest. Just what I needed. She told me if I do this, this, and this it will work. If I don't, it won't. Pretty simple actually. And then, the big kicker, she approached me about co-writing a cookbook. A cookbook. Me, co-writing a fitness cookbook. That had been a dream of mine for years. When she asked me to do this I was just a month into cleaning up my act. She saw something in me that I wasn't seeing yet so I took on the challenge, scared, but excited.

That was the missing piece. I have worked since that day developing healthy, whole food recipes, for my family and me. And that was exactly what I needed. I am a good cook and I grew up learning how to cook from my mother who is an amazing cook. I even worked briefly as a sous chef at a Dude ranch. I am just not afraid of experimenting in the kitchen. I love it and hope you will too.

Why Write This Book?

"Food is our common ground, a universal experience."

James Beard (1903-1985)

Why did we write this book? Well, we had to write it! Obesity is a rising epidemic; people all over the world are increasing their waist size and decreasing the size of their wallets trying to buy the quick answer to long term fat loss. Jamie and I wanted to show the world real solutions without gimmicks and trial size offers. To give people real meal choices which are designed to be healthy *and* tasty. These recipes are "clean foods" which will help keep your insulin levels even, feed your muscles and give you balanced nutrition at the same time. If you just replace your old eating habits with healthy choices as well as become more active for 30 minutes a day you will be looking at a successful fitness journey. We are real people who have managed to reach real results with our fitness journey. We are presenting the tools we ourselves use to achieve the results many people are seeking. There are no quick answers to this epidemic. You did not gain the fat you want to lose over night and you won't lose it over night either.

As we explained in the previous chapter, we know what it is like to struggle with fat loss, with fitness goals and the desperation one can feel to just look normal. You can't just wake up one morning with no plan and no knowledge and become healthier. Jamie and I each began with a mind set and desire. I know you have the same desire or you would not have purchased this book. So with that desire you have a goal. Your goal is individual and it will change and evolve along your fitness journey. A goal is important and a tangible tool to be used to help you along the way. So right now set your goal, or vocalize your goal. Write it down on a piece of paper, on an internet blog, with soap on the bathroom mirror if you have to. Be specific with that goal; don't say vague remarks like "I want to lose weight" Be specific, I would like to wear a size....., I want to look like....., etc. Read that goal and KNOW the goal.

When you are tempted to eat that high fat heavy calorie pizza or that ice cream, ask yourself, "How much closer to my goal will I be if I eat that food?"

Every goal has to be backed by a plan. A tangible, reachable goal has to be matched by a plan which can be applied. Some people tout that all things are possible if you apply yourself hard enough. Well, that sounds wonderful, motivational and inspirational but I guarantee no matter how hard you focus and how hard you apply yourself you will not be able to jump to the moon. So, you have to set reachable goals or you will burn out trying to get even half way to the unreachable ones. On that note, let's talk about realistic goals and unrealistic goals. The word goal is defined as; a place in which something moves towards as well as the finish line at the end of a race. If I were to tell you I wanted to jump to the moon you would laugh at me, wouldn't you? Well, perhaps some of you would just pat my arm and wish me luck in my endeavors but you would know it was not a feasible goal to set. What if you were my neighbor and every morning you woke up to see me on my trampoline jumping and reaching and grasping trying in earnest to jump to the moon. I would imagine you would feel sympathy towards my attempts, or perhaps some humor in my seemingly ridiculous challenge. Well, now imagine that this same story line applies to weight loss endeavors.

Obviously this book is about part of the plan; you knew that. If you did not know that and this book was perhaps loaned to you by a friend or you picked it up off the shelf to look busy don't set it down yet! Keep reading and see if you find anything of value in here. Some of you have planned out diets to reach impossible goals. You have given up every food item the magazine articles have told you; you have purchased every last bit of exercise equipment you have seen on the 2 a.m. infomercials all in hopes of reaching this grand goal of a perfect body in 90 days or your money back. So, let's get on with it.

The diet industry is a billion dollar a year industry. It is the single most marketed product in the world. When we turn on the TV we are bombarded with images of thin women with shapely legs and hips and happy white teeth and shiny hair. We see magazine articles with perfect figures and images which promise happiness and contentment with the new diet aide. Hey, this marketing approach works. How often do you see commercials of real women, average women in average clothes with average kids, cars and husbands? Men who have a bit of a paunch belly who are not touting something stupid or seemingly uneducated. Have you yet to see a commercial with a woman who has stretch marks and chubby thighs advertising her new smooth legs from the quality razor she uses? Of course not, because reality doesn't sell.

Women are shown continuously that we need to be thin, flawless and airbrushed in order to bring attention and happiness to ourselves. Men are shown with a rugged 5 o'clock shadow and chiseled abs on cologne commercials and underwear ads. That is where the flaw in the goal lies. We set our goals to look like the gorgeous model in the ad who tells us that she too had unsightly fat clinging to her hips and thighs. They encourage us with a whitened smile and airbrushed mid section to purchase this amazing new product while supplies last.

These products are not real, nor are the results.

You won't find plastic surgery in a bottle. No matter how many calories you restrict, no matter how many meal plans you buy or how much exercise equipment you purchase you will not be able to jump to the moon.

So, here we are offering you a few tools to use to make a realistic life style change. Your goals will be attainable and your results will be real, not air brushed. We are going to show you real foods with easy to prepare recipes to help you build a failure proof lifestyle change.

Okay, so now you have your goals mapped. Your plan is unfolding so, let's talk a bit about mind set. If you begin today, right now, this very moment, you have to make a successful thought process your best defense. Tell yourself you can do this, that there are no limits to the success of your desires. If you want to lose weight, even if it is a large amount, tell yourself this is it, "I WILL REACH MY GOALS! " You will not use words like "try" "attempt" or other self limiting phrases which have given your mind the permission to let your body fail. Get an image in your head of how you will look when you use the tools you know you have in order to lose the weight you need to lose. Picture yourself at your goal; say to yourself, "I WILL BE AT MY GOAL! I WILL LOOK GREAT AND FEEL EVEN BETTER!" It is all in your head; all the power is right there between your ears. You just have to tell your body IT'S ON! I lost 80 pounds of fat and I am the same person you are. I do not have anything different than you; I just put it all together and made the plan work for me. I wanted it, I worked for it and I achieved it, and so can you.

Key things to remember as you begin your fitness journey:

It won't be over night, it will be trial and error discovering what works best for your body for weight loss. It will be a journey of discovery and adventure. It will teach you more about yourself than you already know.

THERE IS A SUPER HERO INSIDE OF YOU, THERE REALLY IS. ALL YOU HAVE TO DO IS LET IT OUT.

Carbohydrates

If we could give every individual the right amount of nourishment and exercise, not too little and not too much, we would have found the safest way to health."

Hippocrates

Here is some information on what foods do to our bodies. First let's go over carbohydrates. Carbohydrates can be thought of like this: sugar and starch. Bananas, pears, apples, oranges, honey, table sugar, potatoes, grains, candy, bread and pasta are all carbohydrates. Carbohydrates are broken down through digestion into glucose molecules. When used as energy, carbohydrates become fuel for your muscles and brain. If your body does not have any use for the glucose, it is converted into glycogen and stored in the liver and muscles as an energy reserve. Your body can store about a half a day's supply of glycogen. **If your body has more glucose than it can use as energy, and enough has been converted to glycogen for storage, the excess is converted to fat.**

Our body coverts carbohydrates into glucose, our primary energy source. They are *critical* for brain function and red blood cell function. We need carbohydrates to fuel our muscles as well as our daily activities. Carbohydrates are an important fuel source and should not be ruled out of the diet. I am sure you have heard the term "impact carbs" thanks to the new diet craze of "low carbing" it. Low impact foods are foods which slowly convert to glucose and keep the blood stream fed at a steady pace with this energy source. Foods like whole grains or foods closest to "natural" like brown rice are great "low impact" carbohydrates. They take longer to digest so the glucose is released at a slow and steady pace. One of the main reasons why they take so long to digest is because of fiber. We will go over fiber separately because it is so important and fun to talk about! Okay, well important anyway.

The carbohydrates you want to avoid or at least limit are those which cause a quick spike of glucose in the blood. It is essentially a sugar rush. Your blood stream has a fast increase in blood sugar which increases the need for the body to even out the levels. Now stay with me here.....Your body does not KNOW this is a quick rush of glucose, for all it knows this is how life is going to be forever. A constant rush of glucose in the blood needs to be used. It is there for a reason. So the cells absorb the glucose as fast as they can (thanks to insulin) so each cell is force fed this energy food. Now, if this energy is not used, our body is not going to waste it! We convert it to fat to be used as an energy source later....see how easy this is? Also, with the quick spike, remember our body thinks this is how life is now....so when the glucose is used up and there is no longer a huge rush in our blood stream our body starts to slow down. We are conserving energy now because the glucose energy source is gone. This explains the slow down in the afternoon for a lot of people. The cravings for a cookie or some chips at night when we are tired are all ways the body says HEY BUDDY GIVE ME A RUSH!! There are some foods that many people do not realize are in this category, things like bleached flours (yes all the products made with white flour can fit in this quick rush category), white rice, as well as noodles (yes this means pasta). Read your labels. If the ingredients say things like "enriched" run away. This means the good whole grains have essentially been broken down and the nutrients in them are dead. So the makers of food decided, "Hey, if we call it enriched and add in artificial "nutrients" people will presume it is better." Now to look at this closer, this is like eating partially digested foods with a multi vitamin added in. If I handed you food that I chewed really well and almost swallowed would you eat it? I would hope not, but this is essentially what these processed white flour laden products are. Think about that fact next time you are perusing the bakery aisle. Better yet, stay out of the bakery aisle.

So now you know what carbohydrates do in our body and why we want the most natural forms of foods. The easier it is for the body to digest it, the higher the glucose spike. Foods which have had the fiber removed like wheat flour are "partially digested" for you. Foods which are more substantial, like whole oats, whole grain bread and foods that look as close to the form they were in when they sprung from the earth take longer for the body to digest so the glucose level is steady and even. Making it even more simple, if it says on the package "cook and eat in under 3 minutes" picture the rush of glucose, the cells of your entire body gulping quickly in order to balance out and then the stuffed over full feeling after too much thanksgiving dinner…..in every cell of your body….then the amount of fat this will convert to….all because we wanted dinner in under 3 minutes.

So now that you know which carbohydrate foods won't be in our recipes, let's go over the ones that will be there! We don't want you to fear carbohydrates as a food group. There are great sources of food, rich with complex carbohydrates that so many people avoid thanks to this low carb craze. Healthy carbohydrates help us to store energy in the muscle cells to fuel our workouts. Carbohydrates also become stored energy in our liver that feeds us energy throughout the day. I have had people ask me if they should avoid carrots, onions and fruits because of the carb-phobia of the new millennium. I ask you this have you ever met a person who was over weight who told you they got that way from eating too many carrots? Think about that for a moment. Fruits and vegetables are rich with fiber, vitamins and minerals. We are biologically designed to need the nutrients those foods provide so, we need to eat them. If we avoid these foods we will become malnourished.

Whole grain sources are also rich in fiber and the nutrients our body needs. When we cook with foods like brown rice or sweet potato or even oatmeal, we will be fueling our body correctly and we won't have that sluggish tired feeling every afternoon that so many people experience. Also, adequate and proper carbohydrate consumption protects our body from using our muscles as energy. We would not want to lose our muscle in order to avoid a baked potato, right? After all, our muscle is a metabolically active tissue in our body which burns calories all on its own, so let's keep what we have!

Here are some examples of healthy carbohydrate choices you can look for on your next quest to the market as you plan out the meals to begin your fitness journey.
Old Fashioned Rolled Oats
Steel Cut Oatmeal
Brown Rice
Whole Grain Pasta
Stone Ground Wheat Bread
100% Whole Wheat Bread
Whole Fruits
Whole Vegetables
Legumes

Now let's go over water and fiber. We can't discuss fiber without discussing water because the two work as a team in our body. Water and fiber work to keep our body clean and fresh, flushing out toxins in our intestines, from our blood stream and even from our skin. Toxins can interfere with everything our body does. Elimination of toxins from the body will not only help prevent disease and illness but may relieve the body from ongoing ailments as well. From acne to cancer, toxins are believed to be the cause of imbalance in our bodies. Build up of toxins interferes with our basic body functions. If you add any ingredients to a machine which do not belong in that machine a decrease in performance will be seen. Adding more and more toxins without relief can eventually cause this machine to cease running at all.

Improper function of the intestines allows the toxins to sit and wait, only to be reabsorbed by the blood stream and distributed throughout the body. This is where fiber is important! Fiber helps keep your digestive tract tuned up by cleaning your intestines. Water works with the fiber to help fill you up faster and keep things running smoothly for you. This cleansing action can affect your entire body. If your nutritional food is absorbed without interference, you will reap the benefits of a healthier diet. Your body will get what it needs and eliminate what it doesn't need.

The kidneys expel waste from the liver. When the kidneys fail to work properly there is again an overload of toxins free floating in the blood stream. Fluids build up and cause problems with the whole function of the body as well. Wow, that sounds terrible, doesn't it? You can just picture the whole mess inside of you! What could be the answer to this perilous situation? Will there be a rescue to our impending doom? Oh, sorry...drink water. Water keeps the filter functioning. Water makes the world go round! (literally but that is another topic)

Talking a little bit more about the water – fiber love connection. A form of fiber which works best with water to fill you up is called soluble fiber. Soluble fiber forms a gel like substance which is not absorbed in the body at all. It binds with fatty acids to reduce fat absorption. It slows the food digestion in the stomach itself which allows for a more even blood sugar impact. (No crash and burn effect from carbohydrates.) It has been documented to help reduce blood cholesterol levels as well. This fiber works with water so you need to drink your water to help this fiber work. Otherwise you're a car with a full gas tank but no keys to make you go! Oats, bran, apples, oranges, carrots Oh MY! Those are all good sources of soluble fiber and are readily available to you!

Insoluble fiber does not absorb water and works more as the muscle in the fiber family. It helps move foods along, helps balance the PH of the intestines (which helps prevent colon cancer). Let's face it, it keeps you regular. If you are reading this book you are interested in improving your appearance and your health and you know the importance of this so stop giggling and looking around to see who is watching you read about fiber. Water works here to help keep things moving along as well. Water is the Yin to fiber's Yang. Good, readily available insoluble fiber sources can be as wonderful as fruit skins, green leafy vegetables, green beans, broccoli, and cauliflower....think garden here. As a side note, isn't it funny how these food sources are also loaded with water...funny how nature works like that.

Don't worry right now if you are not getting enough fruit and vegetables. Make sure to get the minimum of 5 servings of fruits and veggies a day, your 4-6 servings of whole grains a day and your 8-10 glasses of water a day. Avoid processed foods like fruit roll ups and eat apples. Instead steer clear of white bread and opt for whole wheat (again, not enriched flour either, read the labels)!

So, there you have it. One of the most over looked but vitally important and incredibly easy ways to feel fuller and healthier. Now, you can set this book down and run to the store for an apple and some water. Go ahead; we will be here when you get back.

PROTEIN

If we are what we eat, what do we want to be? Well, for me, I want to be lean and strong. I can't think of one person who wants to be soft and lumpy with globs of fat on them. So in the previous chapter I covered how carbohydrates work in our body and why we can gain fat from them and how we can think of them in a better light. Now, let's talk about protein. We know we have muscles, at least you should know that by now. We also know muscle is made up of protein. Protein is made up of amino acids which are the building blocks of muscle. Proteins are broken down into their constituent amino acids during digestion which are then absorbed and used to make new proteins in the body. Certain amino acids can be made by the human body. However, the essential amino acids cannot be made. So, they must be supplied in the diet. The eight essential amino acids required by humans are: leucine, isoleucine, valine, threonine, methionine, phenylalanine, tryptophan, and lysine. For children, histidine is also considered to be an essential amino acid. Muscles are formed and repaired from amino acids. Muscle in turn requires a constant supply of amino acids (protein) because they are always being used, broken down and rebuilt, every day of the year. In fact, proteins play a crucial role in virtually all biological processes in the body. All of our enzymes are proteins which are vital for your body's metabolism. Our immune system and the messages sent out and received by our nerve impulses are all dependent on proteins. Proteins in skin and bone provide structural support. Even some of our hormones are proteins. Protein can also provide a source of energy when carbohydrate sources are too low as we showed previously. Even reaching for the remote control requires a bit of muscle to be used. Our muscle makes up *at least* 15% of our body weight, in fact. If we do not eat enough protein, we lose muscle…simple as that. We know muscle increases metabolism, we know muscle helps us burn more calories all day long. So, muscle is something we DON'T want to lose.

Now, unlike carbohydrates, protein is NOT stored in the body for later use. In order to have adequate amino acids available to replenish the muscle we use through out the day we need a constant supply of it in our meals. Another benefit to protein is it takes more energy for our body to digest, so even in eating it we increase our metabolism. Protein also slows the digestion of carbohydrates so our blood sugar levels stays on an even keel when we have a balanced meal of protein and carbs.

The RDA (Recommended Daily Allowance) is considered too low in protein requirements according to American College of Sports Medicine. ACSM suggests a full gram of protein per lean body weight per day, in active adults. Since you are about to embark on your fitness journey you will become active and you will require more protein.

A key to healthy eating is to find lean proteins, without all that animal fat to clog our arteries and cling to our inner thighs. Look for lean cuts of meat like chicken breast or turkey breast. Pork loin, flank steak, lean sirloins are also good choices. Read the food labels on meat and look at the fat content and compare it to the total calorie content. Avoid meats which are more than 15% fat. Yes, I know these meats are more expensive, but not nearly as expensive as cardiac surgery. Not nearly as costly as treating any of the obesity related diseases at all! In fact, when you compare the costs of eating right compared with dying from obesity, eating right is an easier choice. Why spend your 401K on heart medications when you could spend it on the beach in Hawaii?

A less expensive source of lean whole proteins a lot of people choose are egg whites. You can use egg whites in so many ways so stop picturing the plain scrambled whites on your breakfast plate. As we promised we are going to show you how to prepare foods to be pleasing, egg whites included.

There are ways to save money on the more costly meats. I buy skinless boneless chicken breasts in bulk from my local butcher. Yes, we have a local butcher, and I am sure if you search your yellow pages you will find one as well. Some butcher shops will offer a lower price for bigger orders. I purchase my chicken in 10 pound bags for only $1.99 a pound. This alone is LESS than that 85% ground beef you have been using because it was on sale, right?

Vegetarians are not left out of this protein extravaganza; they just have to do a little more leg work. All they need to do is combine foods with the right amino acids in them to build what is called "complete proteins" e.g. beans and rice. Soy is also a rich protein source for vegetarian fitness enthusiasts. Protein powders can also be used by vegetarians to sprinkle into foods to offer the benefits of a complete amino acid mix. We have included several recipes with protein powder that are actually so good your kids will love them!

So to recap, protein cannot be stored in the body but our body is in constant need of amino acids for cellular repair to muscle tissue. If we eat protein with every meal we are meeting the nutritional needs of our body, we are slowing the digestion and impact of the carbohydrates in our meal, and we are increasing our metabolism with the meal simply by digesting the protein. So this is a WIN -WIN, right?

Fats

Now we need to look at dietary fats and fads. In the 1990's a new era of fat theory came into the diet scene. New products were rampant with no fat, low fat and negligible fat labels. Low fat diets were said to prevent cancer, prevent heart disease and promote weight loss. I mean, it is simplistic isn't it? If we are what we eat and we see we have gained fat it must be FAT making us fat. Wrong.

Research conducted at Harvard and reported in the Journal of American Medical Association proves that it is not the amount of fat in the diet but rather the **type** of fat in your diet that prevents disease and weight loss. An 8 year study showed there was no prevention of heart disease, cancers or even weight loss with a group of women who ate a low fat diet.

What research has shown is that the good fats like monounsaturated and polyunsaturated fats lower the risk for disease while bad fats like trans and saturated are shown to increase the risk of disease. So the key is to find good fats.

Fat has an important role in a successful fitness journey eating plan. Fat gives the digestion something to do. It takes longer to digest fat and it makes you feel fuller longer. We need fats for energy, insulation and for regulating our hormones and metabolism.

Animals store their energy in fat. Animal fat is known as "saturated fat". If our diet contains too much saturated fat we can accumulate cholesterol and triglycerides in our blood. As we know, these are the substances that clog our arteries and are a leading cause of heart attacks and stroke. However, beef contains a fatty acid called stearic acid. Studies have shown that stearic acid can reduce the "bad" cholesterol in the blood. This just shows that moderation with red meat is the key and that ruling it out is not needed in a clean kitchen.

Plants store their own energy in unsaturated fats. Unsaturated fats are known as polyunsaturated and monounsaturated. Monounsaturated fats are found in olive and canola oils. Polyunsaturated fats are essential in our diets as our body cannot produce them. Remember fatty acids are needed for normal growth and behavior and help with healthy cell membranes, a well balanced hormone level and properly working immune system. Fatty acids play an important role in the regulation of cholesterol levels, and are precursors of prostaglandins, hormone like compounds producing various metabolic effects in tissues. You need essential fatty acids to regulate lung function, blood flow and immune function. Don't eliminate all fats from your diet...let's look at good fats! One of the most crucial polyunsaturated fats is linoleic acid, an omega 6 fat. This can be found in corn oil, sunflower seeds and oil, as well as in supplement form. The other essential fatty acid is of a similar name, Linolenic acid, the omega 3 fatty acid. You can find this omega 3 in fish oils, nuts, and canola and soybean oils as well as in supplement form.

Clean Foods

Clean Protein Choices

Meat and Poultry	
Beef tenderloin	Skinless boneless chicken breast
Sirloin	Skinless boneless turkey breast
Ground beef EXTRA lean	Low fat turkey sausage
Pork tenderloin	

Eggs and Dairy	
Low fat cottage cheese	Low fat ricotta cheese
Egg substitute	Milk, low fat or skim
Egg whites	Yogurt, low fat, low sugar

Fish	
Cod	Salmon
Crabmeat	Tuna fresh
Halibut	Tuna, canned water packed
Red Snapper	Most all others

Soy and Vegetarian
Soy Milk
Tofu, light

Clean Non-Starch Carbohydrates

Fruits			
Apples	Berries, fresh or frozen	Lemon	Pineapple, fresh
Unsweetened apple sauce	Grapefruit	Lime	Strawberries, fresh
Avocado	Grapes	Oranges	
		Pears	

Clean Non-Starch Carbohydrates, *continued*

Vegetables			
Asparagus	Cucumbers	Mushrooms	Spaghetti squash
Bean sprouts	Cauliflower	Onions	Spinach
Bell peppers	Eggplant	Parsnips	Tomatoes
Broccoli	Green beans	Peas	Turnips
Brussels sprouts	Jicama	Radishes	Yellow squash
Cabbage	Leeks	Rutabaga	Zucchini
Carrots	Mixed greens *(salad greens, beet greens etc)*	Scallions	
Celery			

Clean Starchy Carbohydrates

Vegetables			
Acorn squash	Legumes	Pumpkin	Sweet potato
Corn	Potato		

Whole Grain Carbohydrates

Grains, Bread, and Pasta			
Brown Rice	Oatmeal, *old fashioned*	Barley	Millet
Bulgur Wheat	Quinoa	Wheat Germ	Whole wheat pasta
Oat Bran	Wheat Bran	Whole grain bread	Wild Rice

Healthy Fats

Oils and Nuts			
Canola oil	Sunflower seeds	Flax seeds	Pecans
Olive oil	Walnuts	Avocado	Natural Peanut Butter
Almonds			

** These lists are not complete by any means*

Learning To Cook Efficiently
(Don't Waste Time)

One thing that I would like for you to learn is how to cook in bulk. If you are like me and work full time and have a husband and children, this is the only way to go. A few well planned hours in the kitchen can carry you through a full week of eating 5–6 excellent meals a day. I will show you how to do this. Great tasting foods do not have to be off limits. You have to cook but, it doesn't have to be some big, elaborate time consuming effort. There is no way around it. To eat whole, natural, fresh, real foods many times a day, seven days a week, you have to cook. But, it doesn't have to be difficult.

There is an easy way to think about your meal plan ratios. If you follow a diet that requires 5 meals a day at say 40 % protein, 40% carbohydrates, and 20% fats and you know how many calories you need to eat in a day, you can follow these guidelines. To make a recipe that fits your diet, know how much protein you need in a serving. For example I'm going to make a soup, how about chicken and rice? I eat 5 oz of chicken per meal so if I want to make 4 servings I use 20 oz of chicken for the soup. Okay next thing is the starchy carbohydrate, brown rice. I usually eat 1/2 c per meal so now I need 2 c cooked rice. Everything else in the soup is FREE except for the olive oil to sautee the vegetables. Take your portion of fat, say 1/2 tablespoon, multiply by 4 and you sautee with 2 tablespoons of oil.

Now for the free stuff, add tons of veggies, at a bare minimum, 1 c per serving. So I can add 1 c celery, 1 onion, 1 green pepper, 1 c zucchini and lots more. Now the broth and the seasonings are free too! Add lots of seasonings, whatever you like, cover with broth, and cook for a couple of hours. Voila, 4 servings of a perfectly balanced meal just for you. Now if you had doubled the recipe you could freeze a few servings and have some next week, too. Remember, I'm also cooking for my family so I realistically will get 2 servings for myself and the family will have the rest.

Now apply this simple formula to more soups, stews, chilis and casseroles. When you start cooking items separately you still apply the same principle. If you want to make 5 meals at once just calculate how many ounces of protein, how many servings of a carbohydrate and then add tons of veggies.

Make the recipes fit your lifestyle and your tastebuds. I love to eat really spicy foods but my family refuses. So we compromise. I have learned to make the dish a little spicy and then add the extra kick at the dinner table.

These recipes are a starting place. If you need something different, say 3 more oz. of chicken, add it. Cut the fats down or add more, most of these recipes will work with your ratios. Now the exception to this recipe tweaking is baking. Baked goods require a special chemical balance so try to keep your ratios intact. Experiment and have fun creating healthy meals.

CHICKEN & TURKEY

Spicy Chicken Salad

(2 servings)

9.75 oz. can chicken breast in water
1/2 c salsa
1 T safflower oil mayonnaise
1/4 t garlic powder
4 shakes hot sauce
pepper to taste
1 T sweet onion finely diced
2 T celery finely diced
1 t lime juice

Drain chicken and mix all ingredients together.

SERVE on a big pile of greens topped with 1/4 of a sliced avocado.

Other Good Ideas!

- –Serve with whole grain crackers
- –Stuff a garden fresh tomato with the chicken salad
- –Stuff an avocado with the chicken salad
- –Pile on whole grain toast and fat free cheese and put under the broiler until cheese melts, making a "Chicken Melt"

Nutrition Per Serving

chicken salad only

Calories - 152

Fat - 3.5g

Protein - 23g

Carbohydrates - 7.5g

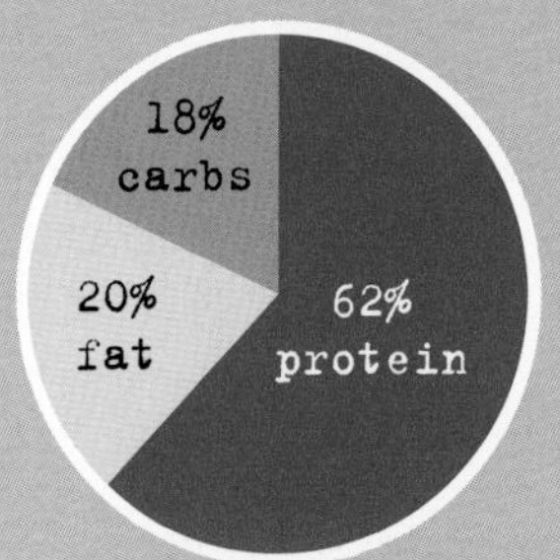

Lemon Chicken

(3 servings)

3 medium chicken breasts 6 oz each

Marinade:
juice of 1 lemon
juice of 1 lime
1 t lime zest
1 T olive oil
2 cloves garlic minced
1 T chili garlic sauce
1 T light mayo

Mix marinade together and put in a zip top baggie with the chicken.

Marinate overnight or for at least 3 hours in the refrigerator. Cook in a skillet sprayed with no stick spray over medium heat. Lightly pepper the chicken before cooking. Cook until browned on the outside and cooked all the way through. Times will vary depending on the size of the breasts. Approximately 25 minutes for total cooking time.

Other Good Ideas!

–Use this chicken in salads, soups, tacos…

–This is really good cold for a picnic

Fresh citrus flavors make this chicken great for salads.

Nutrition Per Serving

Calories - 329
Fat - 11.5g
Protein - 53g
Carbohydrates - 0g

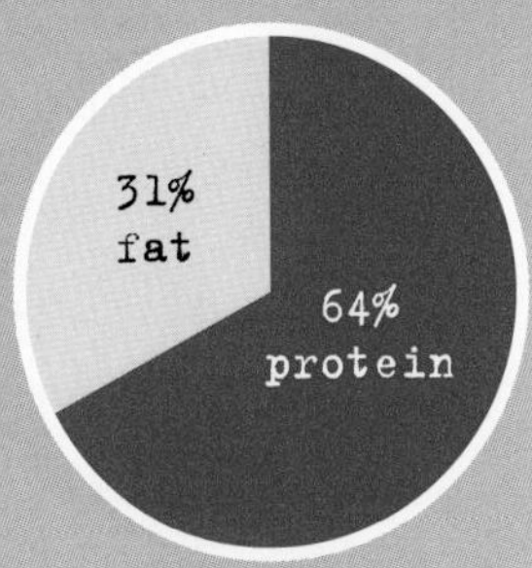

Turkey Burgers
with Sweet & Sour Onions

(4 servings)

1 pound ground lean turkey
1/2 onion diced
8 oz. turkey sausage- breakfast style
1/8 t rubbed sage
5 shakes worcestershire sauce
1 T Onion & Herb blend seasoning
1 t basil
1 t garlic powder
salt and pepper to taste

Mix all ingredients very well in a bowl and form 4 patties. Pepper the tops of the patties.

Cook in pan on medium heat for approximately 25 minutes or until cooked all the way through. Serve topped with the Sweet and sour onions.

Sweet and Sour Onions:
1 medium red onion thinly sliced
sautee onion slowly in a saucepan with;
1 T olive oil
pinch salt
pinch red pepper flakes
2 T balsamic vinegar

Cook over med low heat for approximately 15 minutes stirring occasionally so the onions don't burn or stick to the pan.

Spread generously over the top of the burgers.

Other Good Ideas!

–These onions are good on any grilled meat with a leafy green salad topped with toasted pecans

Nutrition Per Serving

Calories - 330
Fat - 9g
Protein - 52g
Carbohydrates - 7g

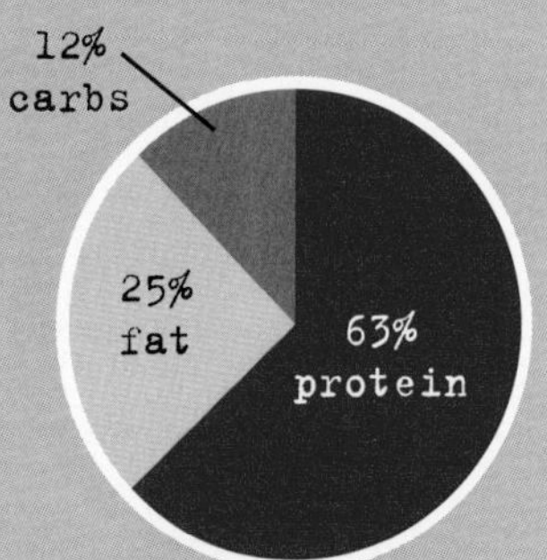

Honey-Lime Grilled Chicken Breasts

(4-6 servings)

1/2 cup chopped fresh basil (4 T dried)
1/2 cup canned low-sodium chicken broth
1/4 cup lime juice
1 T honey
2 t Dijon mustard
2 garlic cloves-mashed
1/2 t salt
dash pepper
4-6 skinless chicken breasts

Combine everything in big zip top baggie. Toss in 4-6 chicken breasts and marinate for at least 3 hours.

Heat your grill to medium heat, turn the heat down then cook the chicken over low or indirect heat depending on how hot your grill is. Over a low heat the breasts will take about 15 minutes or so on each side to get fully cooked and nicely browned. Cook until there is no pink in the center.

Other Good Ideas!

- Add to all of your favorite salads
- Really great with a side of sweet potato fries
- Try to use fresh basil it really makes a difference

This is my family's favorite grilled chicken marinade.

Nutrition Per Serving

approx 6 oz of chicken

Calories - 280

Fat - 6g

Protein - 53g

Carbohydrates - 0g

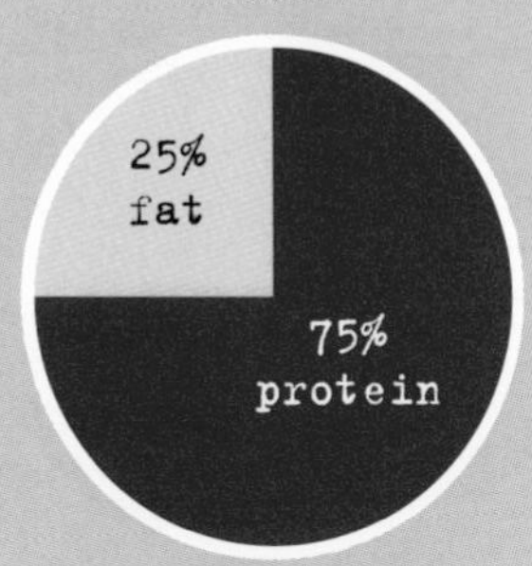

Curried Chicken Salad

(4 servings)

20 oz. cooked skinless chicken breasts
1/4 cup red bell pepper - diced
1 rib celery - diced
3 T onion - diced
1 T jalapeno - diced
1 cup cooked quinoa

Combine the above ingredients in a medium sized bowl.
Now mix the dressing in a small bowl.

Dressing:
1 T mayonnaise
1 T olive oil
salt & pepper
1 t curry powder
1 t garlic powder
1/2 t onion powder
1/4 cup red wine vinegar

Pour the dressing over the mixture and stir to blend everything together. Let the salad sit for at least 15 minutes before serving. Be sure to stir just before serving them over a big pile of baby greens.

Tasty complete meal that everyone will love.

Nutrition Per Serving

Calories - 433
Fat - 11.5g
Protein - 50g
Carbohydrates - 30g

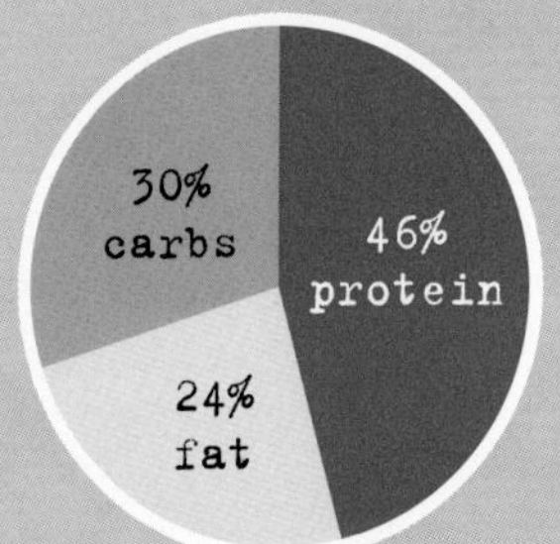

Other Good Ideas!

–This is a great stuffing for a tomato or an avocado

–Food on the go. Just measure your serving into a portable container and remember a spoon. Yummy!

Chicken Soup

(4 servings)

2 large chicken breasts - cooked & chopped
1 T olive oil
1 t basil
1 cup sliced mushrooms
1/2 onion chopped
1/2 t marjoram
3 cloves garlic
1/2 t oregano
1/2 t thyme
1 bay leaf
1 large carrot chopped
1 small zucchini chopped
1/2 yellow pepper chopped
1 14 oz can-no salt diced tomatoes with juice
1/2 cup uncooked barley
4 dashes pepper sauce
2 cans chicken broth
salt & pepper to taste

Heat oil in a large soup pot then add the onion, celery, carrots, garlic and mushrooms. Sauté for about 5 minutes until the onions start to get softened. Add the remainder of the ingredients except the broth and chicken. Bring to a low boil on med high heat then turn the heat down and simmer for 15 minutes. Add the chicken and enough broth to cover all of the ingredients. If there is not enough broth to do this, add some water. Simmer over medium low heat for about 1 hour or until the barley is tender. Enjoy.

Other Good Ideas!

- No carbs? Just omit the barley. Still tastes great
- Try other veggies, fresh tomatoes, summer squash, green beans…

Basic, traditional, heart and soul warming chicken soup.

Nutrition Per Serving

Calories - 346
Fat - 8g
Protein - 40g
Carbohydrates - 28g

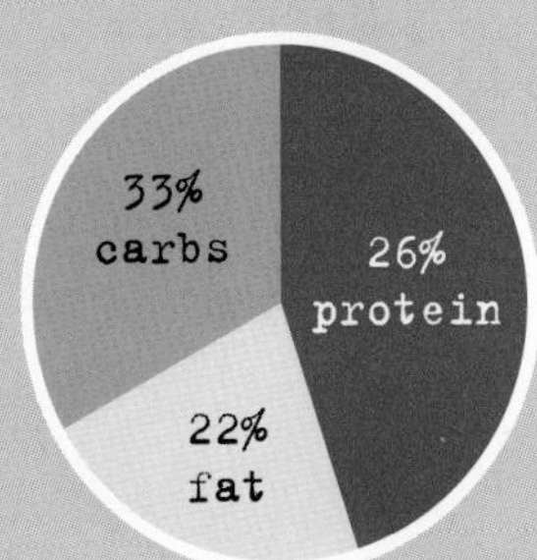

Slow Roasted Chicken

(Servings Depends on the size of the chicken)

---

1 whole chicken that will fit in your slow cooker

- *rinse chicken and pat dry*

coat with 1 T olive oil

Rub all over the chicken, generous amounts of:

lemon pepper, salt, and pepper

or

cumin, garlic and basil

or

Creole seasoning, salt, and pepper

or

Greek seasoning and lemon juice

or

curry powder, garlic, and pepper

or

basil, oregano, pepper, and garlic

Set chicken down into your cooker breast side up. Cook on low heat. Depending on your cooker it may take 4-8 hours to make this bird just fall off the bone. The chicken should shred easily with a fork when it's ready.

This chicken is so easy. Put it on in the morning and it's done when you come home from work.

Other Good Ideas!

–Make pulled chicken sandwiches or chicken tacos with some sauteed onions and peppers

–Chop up the leftovers, add a little of your favorite dressing, some plain yogurt, a few herbs and you have a great salad.

Nutrition
Per Serving

approx 5 ounces of chicken
(white only–no skin)

Calories - 233

Fat - 5g

Protein - 44g

Carbohydrates - 0g

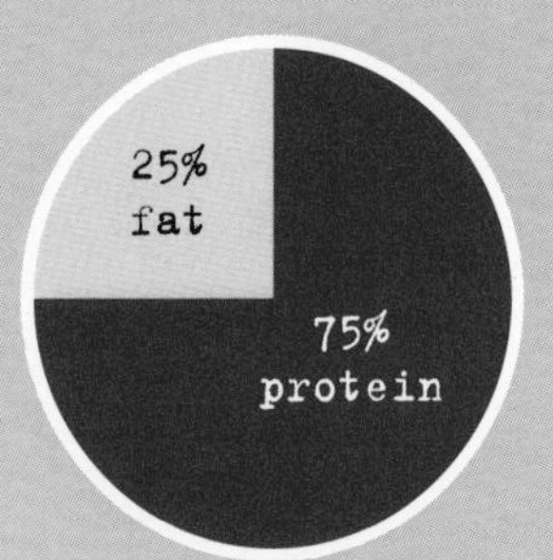

Southwest Chicken Stew

(7 servings)

2 pounds skinless chicken breast *-chopped into 1 inch chunks*
1 T olive oil
1 t garlic powder
1 t onion powder
salt & pepper

Cook chicken in soup pot with the seasonings until done, about 10 minutes on medium heat. Remove chicken from pan and set aside. Reheat pot and sautee:

1 onion chopped
1 red pepper chopped
1 c celery chopped
pinch salt

Cook for 5 minutes then add:

1 bay leaf
32 oz. low sodium chicken broth
2 t garlic powder
2 t cumin
1 t basil
pinch red pepper flakes
1/2 t marjoram
8 oz chopped green chilis *(canned is great)*
1 t paprika
1/2 t salt
pepper to taste
14 oz can tomatoes
14 oz can of beans *(pinto or black, drained)*
1 c water
1/2 c barley

Bring everything to a rapid boil then reduce heat to low and simmer for 1 hour. Or if you want to use a slow cooker, put everything in with cooked chicken and cook on low all day.

Good food for a cold winter day.

Nutrition Per Serving

Calories - 362
Fat - 8g
Protein - 45g
Carbohydrates - 30g

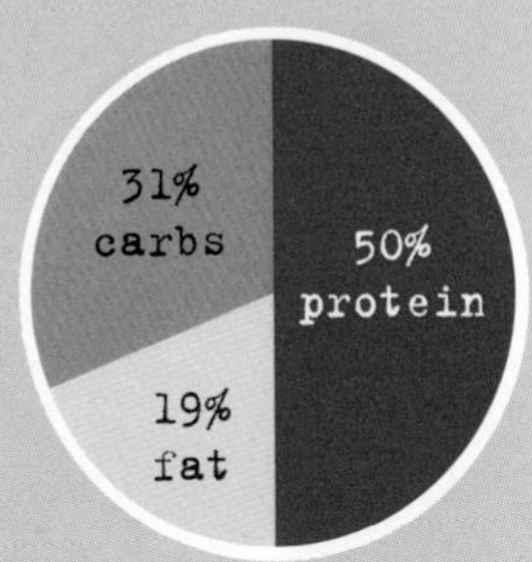

Curried Chicken and Vegetable Stew

(6 servings)

30 oz chopped cooked chicken breasts *(about 3 large breasts)*
1 T chopped garlic
2 T curry powder
1/2 t marjoram
1 onion chopped
1 c carrots chopped
1 c celery chopped
1 c zucchini chopped
15 oz can tomatoes
2 medium potatoes, *chopped to the same size as the vegetables*
32 oz low sodium chicken broth
1/2 t salt
pepper to taste

On the stovetop, sautee the vegetables, but not the potatoes, in 2 T water for 5 minutes on medium high heat with the garlic before adding the rest of the ingredients. Add everything to the pot, bring to a boil then reduce the heat to med low and simmer for 1 1/2 hours.

Slow cooker method. Combine everything in your cooker and cook on low all day. Make sure you just have enough liquid to cover the ingredients.

Invite your friends over for this one. It's so good.

Nutrition Per Serving

Calories - 319
Fat - 6g
Protein - 47g
Carbohydrates - 19g

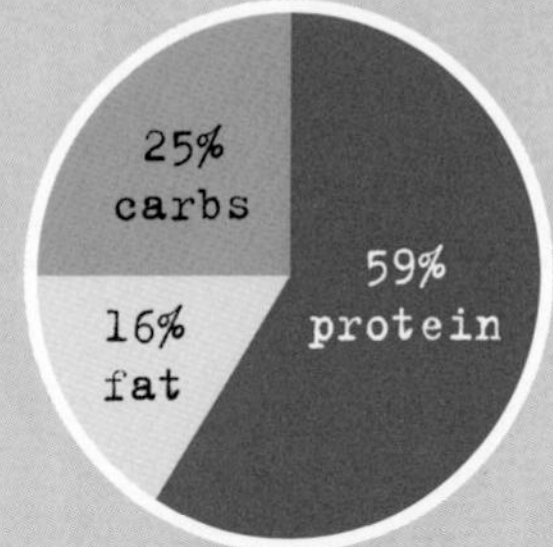

Other Good Ideas!

–Want fewer carbs? Just use one potato and add a little less broth

BBQ Style Chicken

(5 servings)

5 boneless skinless chicken breasts
1/4 c low sodium chicken broth
1 T Dijon style mustard
1/4 c low sugar BBQ sauce
1 t garlic powder
1 t dried basil or 2 T fresh
1 T light mayonnaise or 2 T plain yogurt

Mix everything but the chicken together in a zip top baggie then add your chicken. Marinate 2-12 hours.

Heat your grill to medium heat, turn the heat down and then cook the chicken over low or indirect heat depending on how hot your grill is. Over a low heat the breasts will take about 15 minutes or so on each side to get fully cooked and nicely browned. Cook until there is no pink in the center.

Other Good Ideas!

- Slice thinly and serve over a big salad with avocado
- Chop chicken and add to soups, tacos, casseroles
- Make extra so you can enjoy all week

If you have the time to really cook BBQ chicken, use bone in breasts and this same marinade.

Sweet, Tangy and Amazing BBQ

Nutrition Per Serving

Calories - 292
Fat - 6g
Protein - 53g
Carbohydrates - 3g

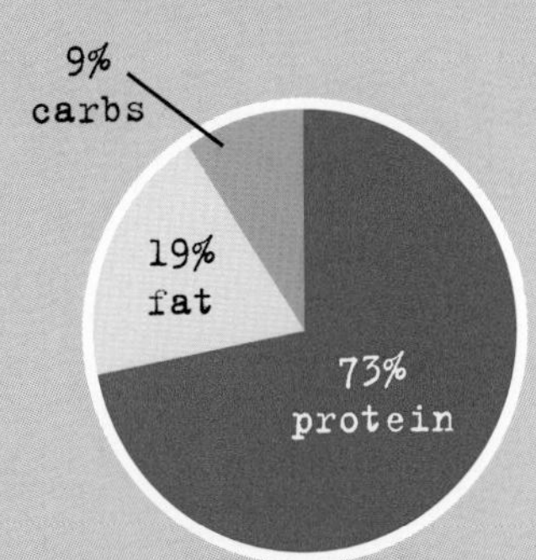

Poached Citrus Thyme Chicken

(6 servings)

6 chicken breasts
1 can low sodium chicken broth
1/2 t salt
1/2 t pepper
2 bay leaves
1 t basil
1 t thyme
3 limes juiced and 1/2 of one of the lime rinds in the pot

Really fast, easy and tasty way to cook all of your chicken for the week.

Add all of the ingredients to a soup pot and cover the chicken with water.

Bring to a boil then reduce heat to medium low and cover the pot. Cook for 10 minutes then let the chicken sit in the hot broth removed from the heat for 20 minutes until thoroughly cooked. Remove chicken from liquid.

Save the remaining broth to make soup.
(Try the Turkey Lime Soup p. 29)

Nutrition Per Serving

approx 5 ounces of chicken

Calories - 233

Fat - 5g

Protein - 44g

Carbohydrates - 0g

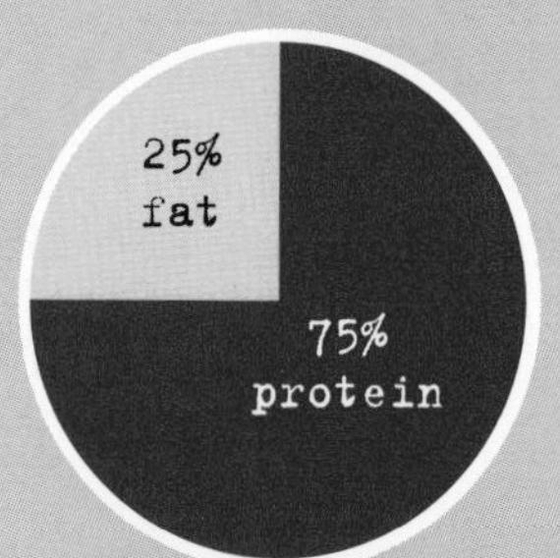

Other Good Ideas!

- –This chicken is great used in salads, soups, and casseroles
- –The lime flavor in the chicken is great for Mexican food
- –Try substituting lemon and orange instead of lime for some different flavors.

TURKEY LIME SOUP

(5 SERVINGS)

Use your leftover stock from the Poached Citrus Thyme Chicken on pg. 28 **or**
2 cans low sodium chicken stock & juice of 1 lime
20 oz leftover cooked turkey chopped small
(chicken is great too)
1/2 onion chopped
1 medium zucchini chopped small
1 can diced tomatoes (14 oz) with juice
3/4 c uncooked brown rice
1 c chopped fresh spinach
1/2 t oregano
1 can (14 oz) great northern beans rinsed
1/2 t marjoram
1/2 t onion powder
4-6 shakes hot sauce

Add everything to the pot except the spinach. Bring to boil on medium high heat then reduce heat to med low and let simmer for 1 hour. Now add the spinach and let cook for another 5 minutes.

LEFTOVER TURKEY? LOOK NO FURTHER.

THIS WILL MAKE EVERYONE HAPPY.

NUTRITION PER SERVING

Calories - 426
Fat - 6g
Protein - 47g
Carbohydrates - 44g

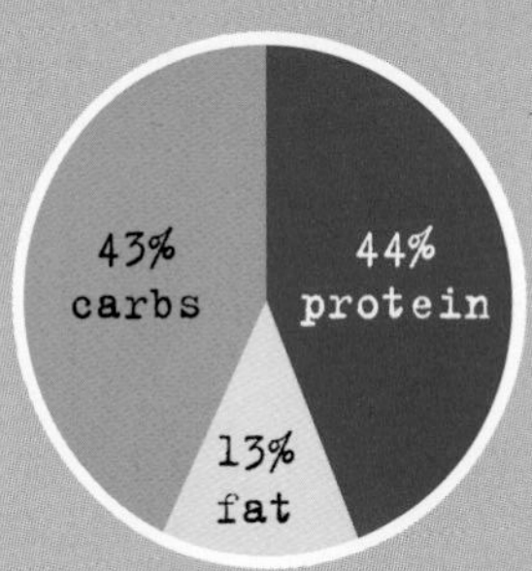

Garlic Chicken on Spaghetti

(2 servings)

10 oz cooked chicken chopped
1/2 onion sliced
1/2 red bell pepper sliced
1 c sliced mushrooms
1 T chopped garlic
1 T olive oil
1 t basil
1 T dry parsley or 3 T fresh chopped parsley
3/4 c roasted garlic salsa
2 T light sour cream (optional)
1/4 c low sodium chicken broth
2 c cooked whole wheat spaghetti
salt to taste

Sauté all vegetables and garlic in the olive oil for 5 minutes over medium heat. Start cooking the spaghetti. Add herbs, salsa and broth and chicken and let cook for another 5 minutes. Turn off the heat and stir in the sour cream. If you want this a little more saucy just add a touch more chicken broth about a few tablespoons at a time.

The spaghetti should almost be done. When it is ready, drain it and measure out 2 cups and add it to the sauce.

Serve in 2 bowls and top with some shredded pepper jack cheese and a spoonful of salsa.

Other Good Ideas!

–Skip the spaghetti and put the sauce on a salad or a pile of spaghetti squash.

A very low carb whole meal.

Nutrition Per Serving

Calories - 587
Fat - 16g
Protein - 57g
Carbohydrates - 56g

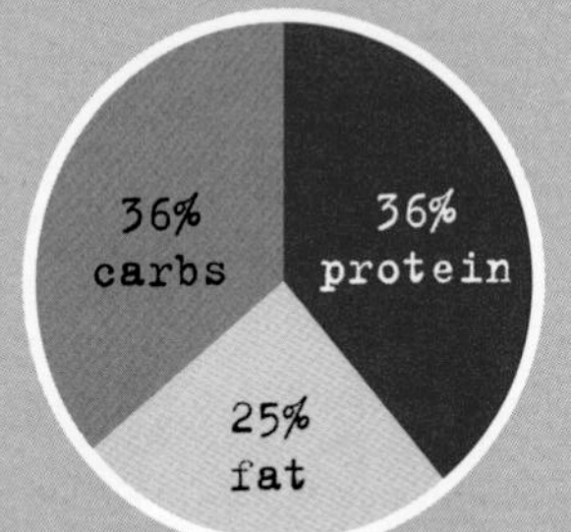

Roasted Creole Chicken

(4-6 servings- depending on the size of the chicken)

1 whole fryer chicken
1 large onion coarsely chopped
2 T olive oil
salt and pepper to taste
2 T Creole or Cajun seasoning
2 t paprika
1 1/2 c sliced mushrooms

Preheat oven to 350 degrees. Rinse chicken and pat dry. Set aside

Chop the onion and put it on the bottom of your roasting pan with the mushrooms. Place the chicken on the onions and rub the bird with olive oil. Sprinkle the chicken generously with the seasonings and don't forget the cavity.

Place into the oven and cook for approximately 20 minutes per pound of bird or until a meat thermometer placed into the center of the thigh reads 180 degrees F.

Remove from oven and let sit for 10 minutes before serving.

Serve the onions and mushrooms along side the chicken.

Other Good Ideas!

- Use on a chicken sandwich with guacamole and thinly sliced onions
- Use this chicken for all of your salads, soups or just serve to your family hot from the oven

Nutrition Per Serving

5 oz of white breast meat without skin

Calories - 233

Fat - 5g

Protein - 44g

Carbohydrates - 0g

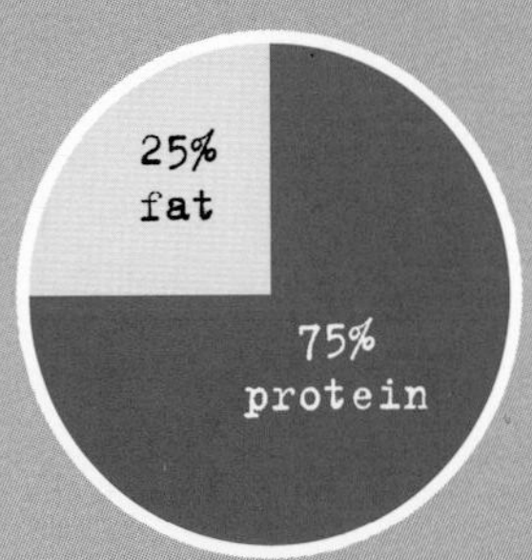

Quick Greek Chicken Salad

(2 servings)

---

10 ounces cooked chopped chicken
4 ribs celery diced
3 pinches dried oregano
5 pinches dried parsley
1/2 t garlic powder
juice from 2 lemons
4 T diced onions
2 T olive oil
salt and pepper to taste

Mix well. Let chill for 15 minutes for a better flavor.

Serve on a bed of fresh raw spinach sprinkled with some toasted pine nuts.

Other Good Ideas!

-Put in a portable container and go, go, go

-Add a serving of cooked barley or quinoa for a complete meal

Nutrition Per Serving

Calories - 369

Fat - 19g

Protein - 44g

Carbohydrates - 3g

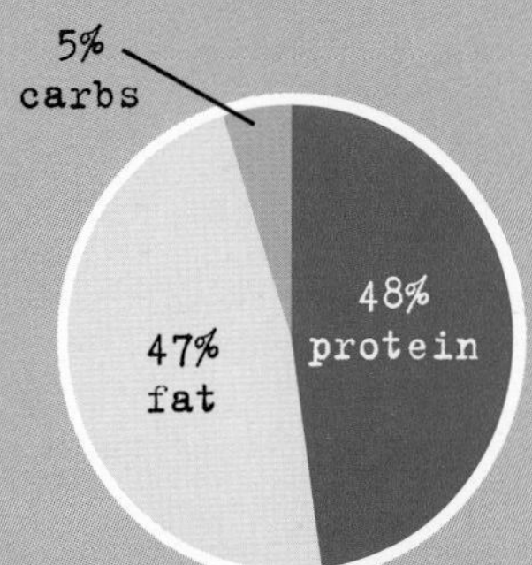

One Pot Tuscan Chicken

(4 servings)

4 6 oz chicken breasts - skinless and boneless
1 onion chopped
3 cloves garlic chopped
1 t basil
1/2 t oregano
1/2 t marjoram
1/2 t thyme
1 t dried parsley
1/2 t rosemary
salt and pepper to taste
14 oz can diced low sodium tomatoes - drained
1/2 carton (2 c) sliced mushrooms

Use a large pot for this. Preheat the oven to 350 degrees. Put the onion and the mushrooms on the bottom of the pot. Place the chicken on top of the vegetables, pour on the tomatoes and then sprinkle well with all of the seasonings. Put a lid on the pot and place in the center of the oven. Cook for approximately 35-40 minutes until the chicken is fork tender and cooked all of the way through.

Serve over brown rice, whole wheat spaghetti, or spaghetti squash if you want a lower carbohydrate meal.

Nutrition Per Serving

Calories - 395
Fat - 7.5g
Protein - 69g
Carbohydrates - 11g

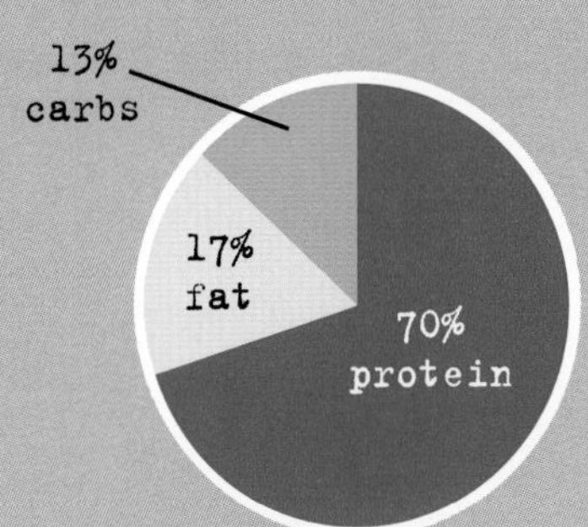

NOTES:

FISH

Sesame Seared Tuna

(3 servings)

2 8 oz. tuna steaks or fillets - 1" thick
3 T soy sauce
1/2 lime juiced
1/4 t salt
pepper to taste
3 T sesame seeds
1/2 lime for garnish

Marinate tuna for 30 minutes in the soy sauce and lime juice. Next coat the tuna with salt, pepper and sesame seeds.

Heat pan and add 2 T olive oil on medium heat. Add tuna and cook approximately 8 minutes on each side. Cooking time may vary depending on the thickness of your tuna. Tuna should be cooked all the way through. Squirt more lime juice on the tuna before serving.

Other Good Ideas!

- Serve with Quinoa with caramelized onions (p. 85) for a fast and special meal
- This tuna is also great cold on a fresh baby greens salad with a light vinagrette dressing

Nutrition Per Serving

Calories - 228

Fat - 6g

Protein -38g

Carbohydrates - 4g

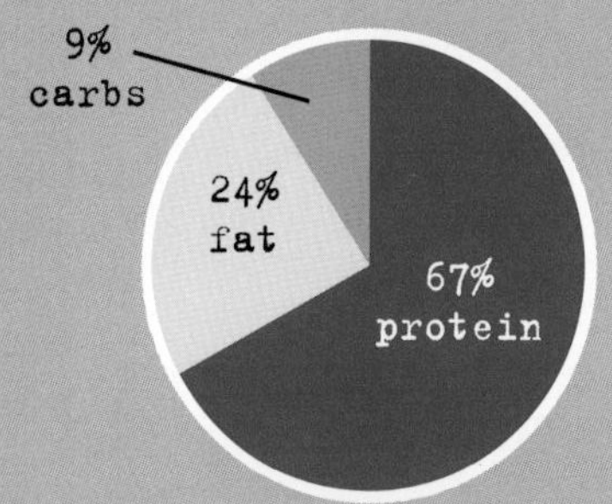

Shrimp & Peppers

(3 servings)

1 1/2 lbs. shrimp - peeled & deveined
1/2 medium onion - sliced
1 each red & yellow peppers sliced thinly
1 t chili garlic sauce
1 T olive oil
3 garlic cloves crushed
1/8 t basil
4 sprigs fresh thyme or 1/8 t dried thyme
1/2 cup chicken broth
juice of 1 lime @ before serving

Heat oil in large skillet over medium heat. Add all ingredients except the shrimp and cook until the peppers are tender, about 10 minutes. Now add the shrimp cooking on each side a couple of minutes or until they are bright pink. Careful not to overcook. Squirt on the lime juice before serving.

Serve over brown rice or pasta

Other Good Ideas!

–Wrap in a warm corn tortilla with some shredded cabbage and a squirt of lime juice for a portable shrimp taco

–Makes a great salad

Nutrition Per Serving

fish and vegetables only

Calories - 300

Fat - 9g

Protein - 44g

Carbohydrates - 8g

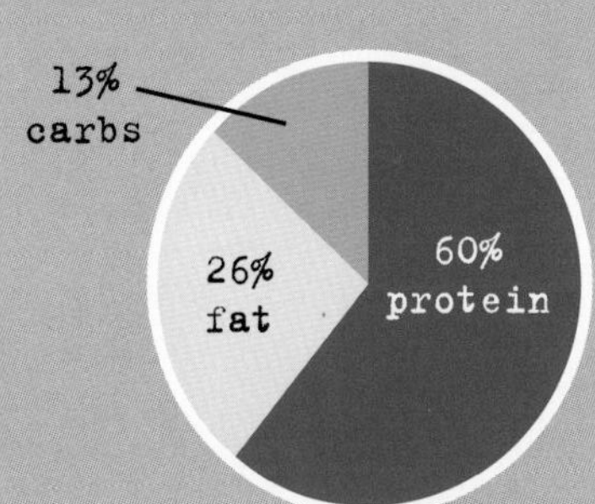

Salmon Croquettes

(3 servings)

1 can (14.75 oz.) salmon
1 egg
1/4 cup oats *(old fashioned)*
1/4 cup onion - diced
1/2 t garlic powder
salt & pepper to taste
1 T green chilis - *canned is okay*
1/2 t Old Bay seasoning
1/2 T olive oil

Drain salmon then put into bowl and flake. Add rest of ingredients except olive oil. Mix well.

Heat non-stick pan on medium heat and add olive oil. Make three patties with the mixture and cook on medium heat approximately 8 minutes on each side until golden brown.

Other Good Ideas!

- These are very versatile for seasonings, mix it up and try what you like
- These are great with some oven roasted broccoli and rice pilaf
- Make tiny croquettes for elegant and healthy appetizers

Nutrition Per Serving

Calories - 263

Fat - 12g

Protein -31g

Carbohydrates - 6g

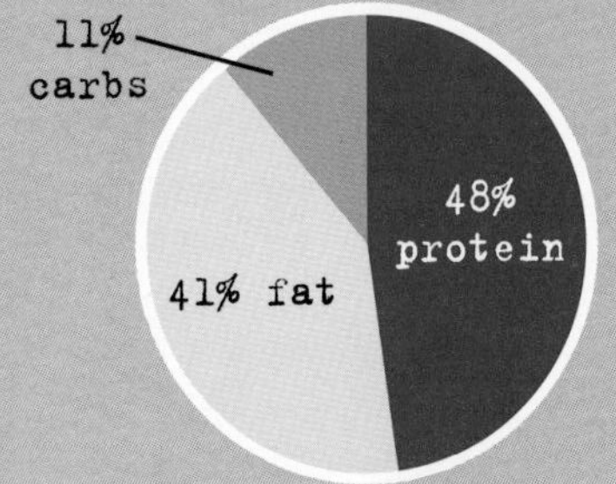

Grilled Trout

(7-9 servings)

---

1 large whole trout, (2 lbs) *cleaned with head removed*
1 lime-juiced
3 garlic cloves minced
1/2 t pepper
2 T olive oil

Make sure your fish is rinsed well and then pat it dry with paper towels. Use 1 tablespoon of oil per pound of fish. Lay out a piece of foil or a fish grill basket and set the trout on it. Drizzle the olive oil on the fish and inside the cavity. Rub the oil all over to make sure it's well coated. Squeeze the lime all over the fish and especially on the inside. Now spread the remaining seasonings evenly on the inside of the fish. Take the allready squeezed lime or a new one if you like and slice several thin slices of the lime and set inside the fish. Preheat your grill to medium heat. Seal up the fish if it is in foil. Now take a knife and make a few slits so the juices gradually run out. (You can skip this step if you like a wetter fish.) Set the fish on the grill and cook about 10 min on each side until the fish is flakey all the way through. Cooking times are for a thick large trout so if you have smaller fish try cutting the time in half.

Sometimes the simplest things are the best. This is my favorite way to prepare the fresh trout we catch all year around.

Other Good Ideas!

- Serve with fresh summer veggies
- Make sure to keep the leftovers to make croquettes. Yum.

Nutrition Per Serving

4 ounces
Calories - 216
Fat - 9g
Protein - 30
Carbohydrates - 0g

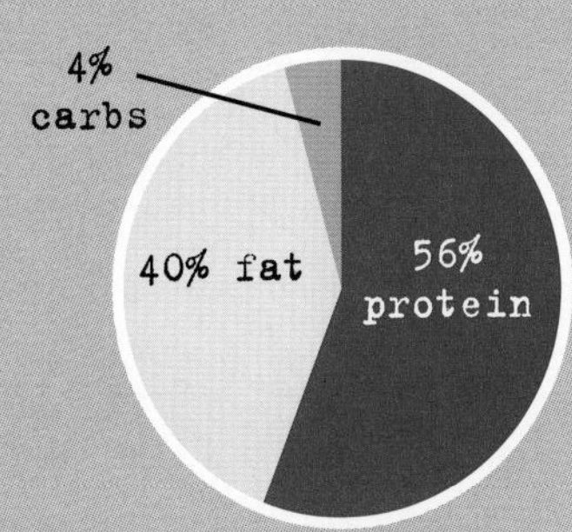

Balsamic & Lime Salmon

(2 servings)

1/2 T olive oil
1 fresh Salmon fillet with skin on one side (1/2 lb)
1/2 lime juiced
1 t chopped garlic or approximately 2 cloves chopped
2 t balsamic vinegar
1 T fresh chopped basil
salt and pepper to taste

Heat up oil in a non-stick skillet to med heat. Lay out salmon and coat with the lime juice and vinegar then spread on the garlic, pepper and basil. Set the fish carefully in the pan skin side up. Cook about 5 minutes then carefully flip the fish over and cook another 5 minutes until flaky and done all the way through. Salt if you want and add an extra squeeze of lime before serving.

Eat your Fish!

Other Good Ideas!

–This fish dish is great hot or cold and goes especially well with lots of fresh salad greens and spinach.

–If you have leftovers, make croquettes or use it just like you would canned tuna. It's just tons better

Nutrition Per Serving

Calories - 206

Fat - 9g

Protein - 28g

Carbohydrates - 0g

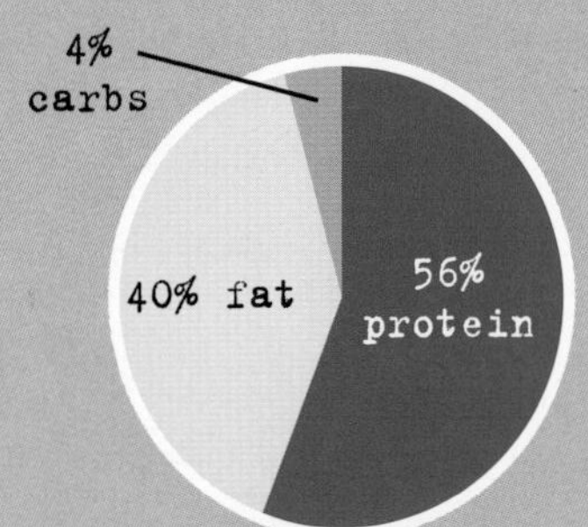

Fresh Great Northern Tuna Salad

(3 servings)

12 oz drained canned tuna- water packed
1 can Great Northern beans- drained and rinsed
2 plum tomatoes diced
1/2 c diced celery
5 sliced scallions
1 lime juiced
2 T olive oil
1 T balsamic vinegar
1 t basil
1 t parsley
salt and pepper to taste

Mix all ingredients together well in a medium bowl and refrigerate for 30 minutes before serving.

Other Good Ideas!

-Put this salad onto a big pile of mixed salad greens for a great lunch or dinner

-Eat just as is for an easy travel meal or take to work meal

Easy, Fast & Fresh Salad

Nutrition Per Serving

Calories - 278

Fat - 2g

Protein - 39g

Carbohydrates - 26g

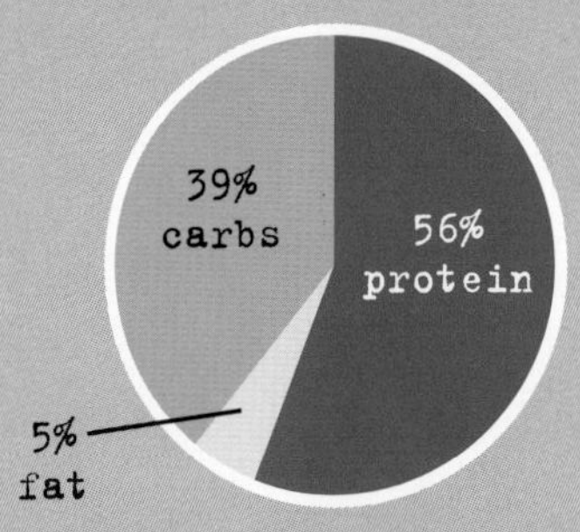

Trout Creole Cakes

(4 servings)

16 ounces flaked cooked trout

(or use any mild white fish like tilapia or snapper)

8 scallions chopped - bottom 3 inches only

1/2 of a sweet red pepper diced

3 eggs or 6 whites

3/4 c old fashioned oats

3 cloves garlic minced

6 shakes hot sauce

1 t Old Bay seasoning

1/2 t paprika

1/2 t Creole seasoning

salt and pepper to taste

2 T olive oil for cooking

1/2 lime for serving

Combine all of the ingredients, except for the oil and lime, in a medium sized bowl and mix really well using your hands. Let sit for 15 minutes or so and then heat 1 T of the oil in a skillet over med to med high heat. Form 8 patties about 1 inch thick with the mixture being careful everything is staying together. Add half of the patties to the pan and cook about 10 minutes on each side. They turn a golden brown when they are done. Be careful when you flip the cakes as they may want to fall apart. Remove from the pan and repeat with new oil. Serve with a squeeze of fresh lime juice.

Other Good Ideas!

–These are excellent hot or cold

–Make tiny ones for party appetizers

Nutrition Per Serving

Calories - 255

Fat - 8g

Protein - 33g

Carbohydrates - 11g

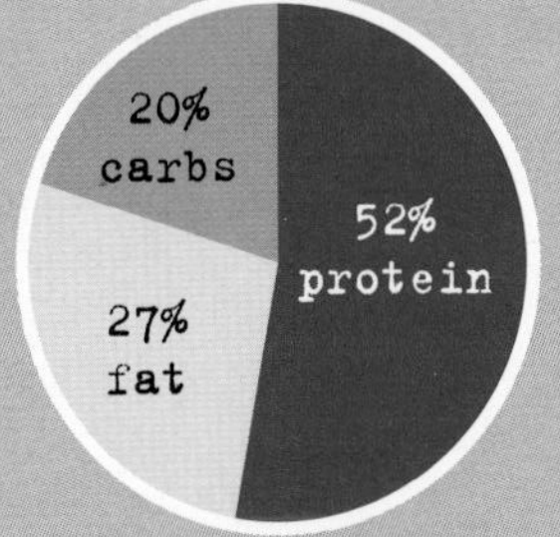

Asian Style Salmon Croquettes

(3 servings)

1 8 ounce can salmon in water-drained and rinsed
1/2 c old fashioned oats
1 T olive oil
1 egg lightly beaten
2 t soy sauce
salt and pepper to taste
1 clove garlic minced
1 t chili garlic paste
1 T black sesame seeds
2 T minced scallions

Mix everything together well except for the oil. Let sit for 10 minutes or so. Heat oil in a skillet then form 4 patties with the mixture. Cook the croquettes approximately 5 minutes on each side., Until golden brown.

Serve with more chili garlic paste on the side.

Other Good Ideas!

–Serve with steamed pea pods and chop sticks!
–This is a dish you can make extra and share at a dinner party
–Make tiny ones and serve as appetizers

Can't think of what to make?

Try these.

Nutrition Per Serving

Calories- 243
Fat - 13g
Protein - 21g
Carbohydrates - 9g

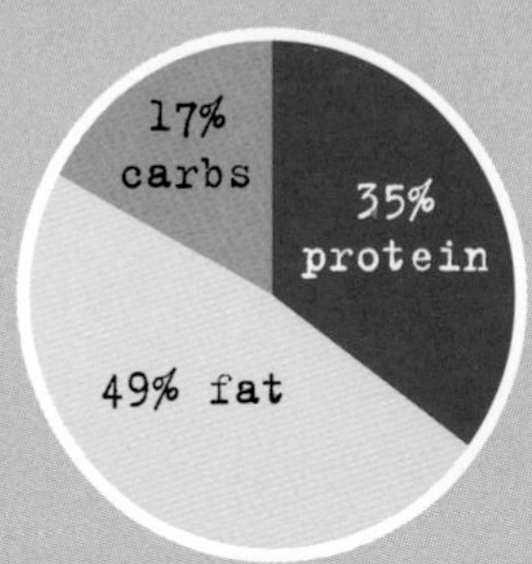

NOTES:

BEEF

Beef and Wild Rice Soup

(5 servings)

Hot, Healthy and Heart Warming.

1 lb lean beef browned
salt & pepper to taste
1 t garlic powder

–Drain off fat if needed & set meat aside.

1 onion chopped
1 c mushrooms chopped
1/2 t salt
1 small zucchini chopped
4 oz can green chilis
1 c cherry tomatoes
1 c celery chopped
1 bay leaf
1 t garlic powder
1 t basil
1/2 t oregano
1 t marjoram
2 t ground cumin
pinch red pepper flakes*–2-3 pinches if you want heat*
2 (14 oz) cans broth*–chicken or beef, low sodium*
1 can diced tomatoes*–no added salt*
1 c water
1/2 c wild and brown rice mixed

Sauté in soup pot- all veggies except for tomatoes for 10 minutes over med heat. Add in rest of the ingredients including the beef. Bring to a boil and then simmer on low heat for 1.5 hours. You may need to add more salt after cooking for a while.

Slow Cooker

This soup can be prepared in a slow cooker. After browning the meat, just toss the rest of the ingredients into the cooker with the meat and cook all day on low. When the rice is tender, the soup is ready.

Nutrition Per Serving

Calories - 344
Fat - 15g
Protein - 30g
Carbohydrates - 21g

25% carbs
35% protein
40% fat

Crock Pot Curry

(6 servings)

1/2 T chili garlic paste
1 T olive oil
2 lbs. beef stew meat
1 can diced tomatoes with juice
3 T curry paste hot or mild or a combination of both
1 t curry powder
1 cup chicken broth
salt and pepper to taste

Add all of your ingredients into the slow cooker and mix well to disperse the paste. Cook on High - 3 hours, then halfway through the cooking add:

2 cups potatoes in chunks
1 cup sliced fresh mushrooms

Serve over brown rice

Other Good Ideas!

-Just use the hot curry paste if you like really spicy curry.
-This gets spicier as it sits in the refrigerator.

This curry is just a touch spicy and is good for the whole family.

Nutrition Per Serving

for just the curry

Calories - 448

Fat - 20g

Protein - 48g

Carbohydrates - 17g

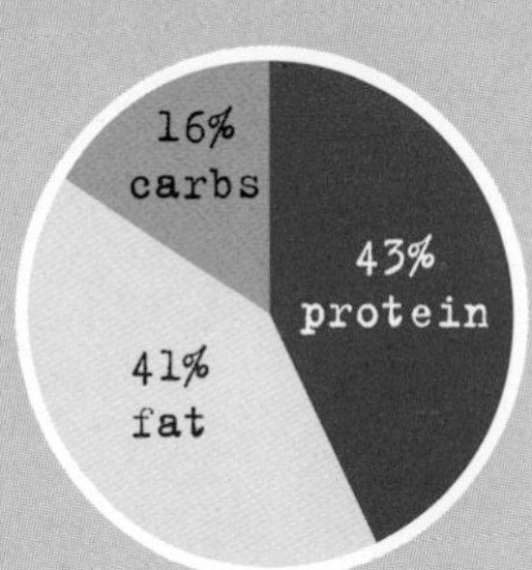

Western States Chili

(6 servings)

1 lb. ground beef - browned
2 c cooked pinto beans
1 T olive oil
1 onion small
1 green pepper
3 medium tomatoes or 1 can chopped with liquid
2 small jalapenos chopped
2 t chili garlic
1 t basil
4 t chili powder
1 t marjoram
1 t oregano
15 oz. canned tomato sauce
1 2/3 cups beef broth
bay leaf
pepper to taste
1/2 t salt

Another hearty, healthy, cold weather meal. Think football parties and cold winter days.

Brown the beef first in a large pot. Drain off any extra fat then add the oil, onion and green pepper and cook for a few minutes. Now add the rest of the ingredients bring to a boil then reduce the heat and simmer for at least 30 minutes.

This chili is also great made with venison.

Nutrition Per Serving

Calories - 346

Fat - 15g

Protein - 29g

Carbohydrates - 24g

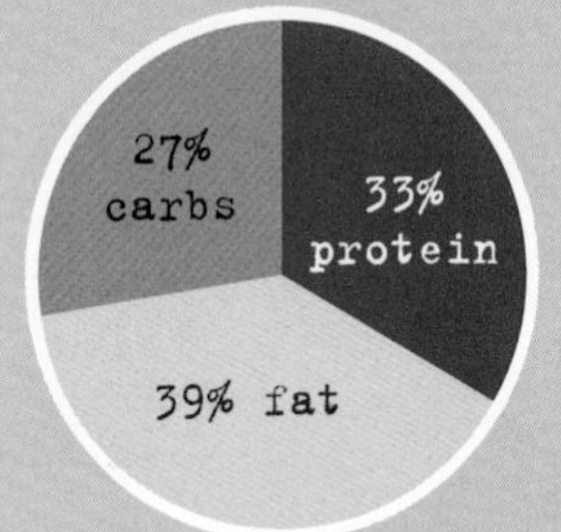

Other Good Ideas!

-Set out toppers for your chili and let everyone pick their own. Some ideas are:

- shredded cheese
- diced onions
- scallions
- low fat sour cream
- avocados

Ropa Vieja

(7 servings)

or Cuban Style Pot Roast

2 medium onions
2 pound beef roast *–your favorite lean cut*
1 carrot - coarsely chopped
1 celery stalk *–coarsely chopped*
1 bay leaf
2 T olive oil
4 garlic cloves *–minced*
2 ajecito chiles *–minced or small can of chopped green chilis*
2 green bell peppers *–chopped*
2 cup fresh plum tomatoes *–seeded & chopped*
1 T dried oregano
2 t cumin
1/4 cup fresh parsley*–chopped*
salt & pepper to taste

Quarter one of the two onions. Put in a large dutch oven or slow cooker with meat, carrot, celery and bay leaf. Cover with water. Bring to a simmer and cook, uncovered, for 1 1/2 to 2 hours. Skim fat frequently (you can also cook all day on low in a slow cooker).

When meat is very tender, remove from broth. Set aside. Discard vegetables and strain broth through a sieve. Return broth to heat, and boil to reduce by half, about 20 - 30 minutes. When meat is cool, cut off any fat and pull into shreds about 2 inches wide.

While broth is reducing, coarsely shop the second onion.

Heat oil in a large skillet. Over medium heat, cook onions, garlic, chiles and green pepper until softened, about 10 minutes. Stir in 2 cups reduced broth and tomatoes. Cook for 15 - 20 minutes over medium heat. Stir in shredded meat, oregano, parsley and cumin. Cook 10 - 15 minutes more.

Serve over brown rice.

Other Good Ideas!

-serve with roasted broccoli for an excellent meal

-this dish is equally good with a tougher cut of meat and slow cooked in the oven

This pot roast is well worth the effort. The flavors are unique but savory and delicious too.

Nutrition Per Serving

rice not included

Calories - 332

Fat - 16g

Protein - 38g

Carbohydrates - 7g

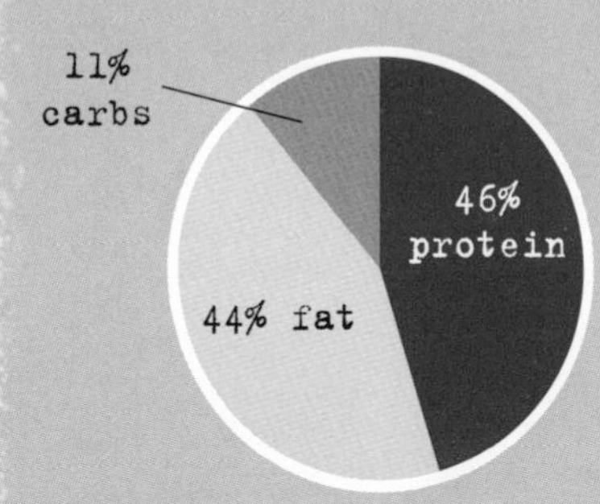

Lime Spiced Steak

(4 servings)

4 1 inch thick steaks, all visible fat removed *(8 oz each)*
2 T dry steak seasoning
juice from 1 lime
2 t ground cumin
2 t chili powder
1 T garlic powder

Mix all of the dry ingredients in a bowl to make a rub. Coat the beef with the lime juice then evenly rub the seasonings on both sides of the meat. Let the meat sit for 15-30 minutes. Using a heavy skillet, heat the pan to med high heat then spray non-stick spray to coat. Add the steaks and cook approximately 5-8 minutes on each side for med to med well cooked. Remove from heat and let sit for a few minutes before cutting.

THIS STEAK IS SUBTLE IN ITS SPICINESS BUT TRULY TASTY.

Other Good Ideas!

- serve with baked potatoes and roasted broccoli for an excellent meal
- this dish is equally good with a tougher cut of meat and slow cooked in the oven

Nutrition Per Serving

using Beef Rib Eye

Calories - 340

Fat - 18g

Protein - 42g

Carbohydrates - 0g

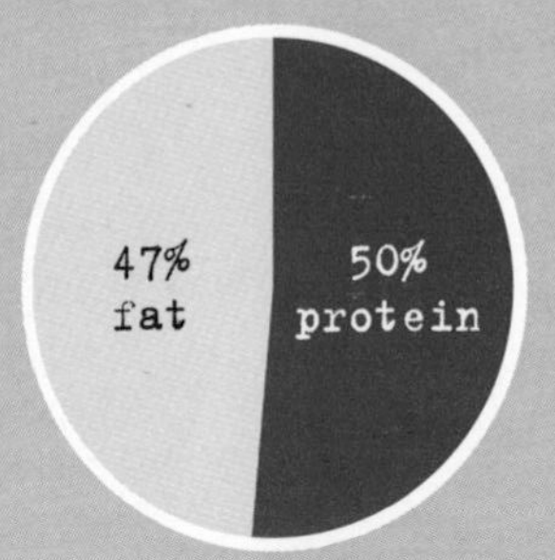

Mexican Burgers
With Onions and Peppers

(7 servings)

1 pound lean ground beef
1 pound lean ground turkey
5 shakes Worcestershire sauce
5 shakes hot sauce
1 T garlic powder
1/2 T onion powder
2 t cumin
1 t chili powder
pinch salt
pepper to taste
1 onion sliced thinly
1 red pepper sliced
1 T olive oil
1/2 t cumin

Mix all ingredients together well in a large bowl. Form 6 patties and season outsides with salt and pepper. Cook on medium heat in a large skillet approximately 15 minutes or until done to your preferance. Or you can grill the burgers outside. While the burgers are cooking, heat the olive oil in another skillet over med heat and saute the onion, pepper and the cumin until tender approximately 5 minutes.

SERVE the burgers with the veggies piled on top.

Other Good Ideas!

-Smooth on some avocado butter for a really special burger

-Serve with some sweet potato oven fries for an excellent meal

THESE HAVE FLAVORS LIKE YOUR FAVORITE FAJITAS ONLY EASIER AND NO STARCHY CARBS.

NUTRITION
Per Serving

Calories - 289
Fat - 17g
Protein - 30g
Carbohydrates - 3g

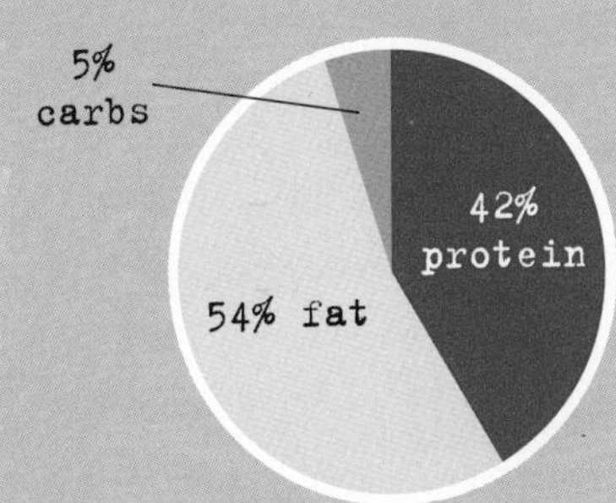

HOUSE GOULASH

(6 SERVINGS)

THIS DISH IS REALLY GREAT COMFORT FOOD. HOT, CREAMY, SAVORY PASTA ALWAYS HITS THE SPOT WITH MY FAMILY.

1 pound lean ground beef
1 med onion chopped
3 c cooked whole wheat rotini or elbow pasta
2 c mushrooms-sliced
1 t minced garlic
1 large can chopped tomatoes with juice
1 T dried parsley
1 t basil
1 t paprika
1 t marjoram
4 shakes Worcestershire sauce
1/2 c light sour cream
1/4 c shredded mozzarella or parmesan cheese

Brown the beef in a large skillet and drain off any extra fat. Put meat into a bowl and set aside. Boil pasta and drain. Sautee garlic, onion, and mushrooms till tender in some of the juice from the canned tomatoes. Add in all of the seasonings and the tomatoes and cook on medium heat for 15 minutes. Add the remainder of the ingredients and cook for another 10 minutes.

NUTRITION PER SERVING

made with mozzarella cheese

Calories - 397
Fat - 18g
Protein - 30g
Carbohydrates - 29g

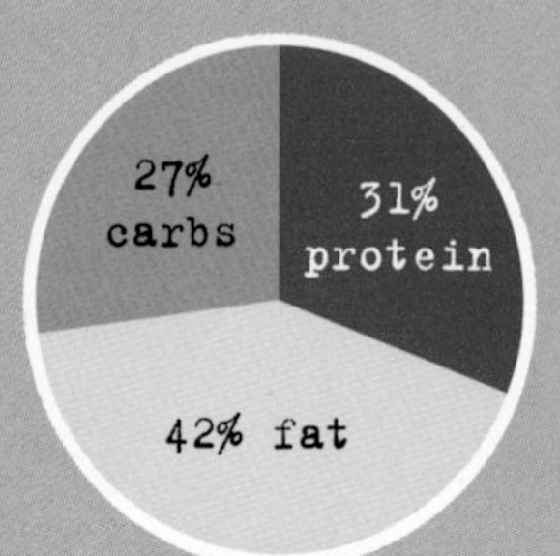

OTHER GOOD IDEAS!

-Vary your seasonings and make this either Mexican with chili powder, garlic and cumin or maybe add curry powder and garlic for an Eastern Indian flair

EGGS, DAIRY & PROTEIN POWDER

MIGAS

(4 SERVINGS)

6 scallions *bottom 4 inches sliced thinly*
4 corn tortillas - *cut into thin strips about 2 inches long*
2 Serrano chilis- sliced *(you can seed the chilis if you want less heat)*
1/3 c low fat shredded cheddar cheese
4 eggs
1 carton egg whites (16 oz) or 14 egg whites
1 tomato seeded and chopped
8 oz turkey sausage- *breakfast style*

How to seed a tomato:
Cut the top off the tomato and squeeze out the seeds over a bowl. Chop the fleshy part of the tomato.

Brown the sausage in a skillet. Remove from the skillet and set aside. Spray skillet with non-stick oil spray to coat pan, then add vegetables and tortilla strips, sauté over medium heat about 4 minutes until the onions have become softer. Add the sausage and all of the eggs and cook like you would scrambled eggs until the eggs are done. Turn off the heat and add the cheese.

SERVE when the cheese is melted. Excellent served with roasted potatoes or potatoes of most any kind.

OTHER GOOD IDEAS!

–Put Migas into a whole wheat tortilla for a portable meal; Voila! Instant breakfast burrito, just add salsa.

MIGAS ARE A TEX-MEX BREAKFAST FAVORITE. SPICY AND COMFORTING AT THE SAME TIME.

NUTRITION PER SERVING

Calories - 300
Fat - 18g
Protein - 28g
Carbohydrates - 4g

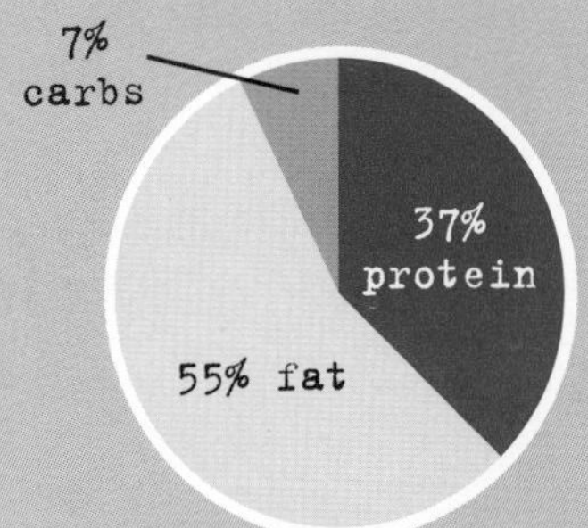

Sunday Morning Eggs

(8 servings)

1 lb. turkey sausage, breakfast style
1 bunch scallions, sliced bottom 3 inches
4 oz can chopped green chilis
1/4 c dry pack sun dried tomatoes, diced
1 t chopped garlic
2 T chopped fresh parsley
32 oz carton of egg whites
3 eggs
1/2 c skim milk
1 c shredded low fat mozzarella cheese
pepper to taste

First, brown the sausage and near the end of cooking add the garlic and the scallions. Add cooked ingredients into a bowl then add the remainder of the ingredients except for the cheese. Pour the mixture into a 13 x 9 x 2 inch baking dish coated with non-stick spray and top with cheese. Preheat oven to 375 deg. Cook for about 30 minutes or until a knife inserted in center comes out clean.

THIS IS AN ELEGANT BUT EASY DISH TO SERVE TO GUESTS. I LIKE TO MAKE THIS FOR BRUNCH ON THE WEEKEND WHEN I HAVE GUESTS IN THE HOUSE.

Other Good Ideas!

–Excellent leftovers

Nutrition Per Serving

Calories - 395
Fat - 24g
Protein - 35g
Carbohydrates - 6g

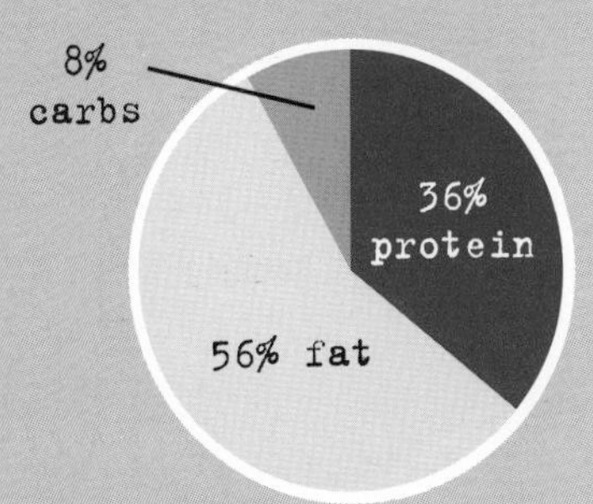

Denver Scramble

(1 serving)

6 egg whites
1 ounce diced ham
2 T diced onion
2 T diced red pepper
1/4 c low fat shredded cheddar cheese

Heat non- stick skillet on med heat and then spray with non-stick spray. Add veggies and ham and cook for a few minutes until onion is softened. Add the eggs and cook like scrambled eggs mixing well. After eggs are cooked, turn off the heat and add the cheese. Serve when cheese is melted.

Other Good Ideas!

–Put in a whole wheat tortilla for a great breakfast burrito

–Serve on salad greens for a light snack

Nutrition Per Serving

Calories - 197

Fat - 4g

Protein - 36g

Carbohydrates - 3g

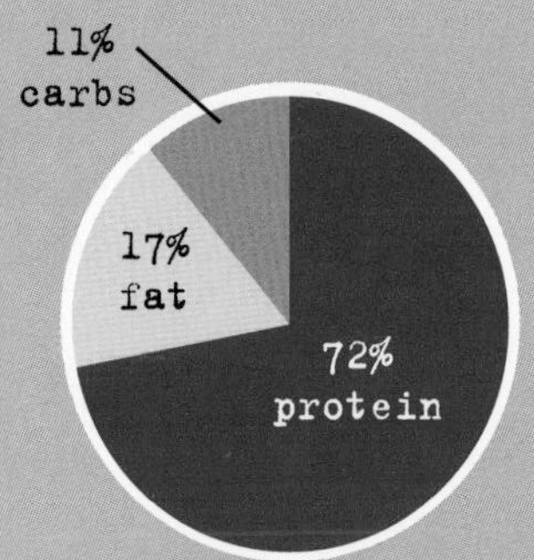

Vanilla Cappucino Shake

(1 serving)

1 c vanilla rice milk or skim milk
1 serving Protein powder- vanilla or chocolate flavor
1/4 t. instant coffee
1/4 t. vanilla
1/4 c ice or more if you want a thicker shake

Blend well.

Tastes like an iced, blended Latte.

Nutrition Per Serving

using egg white protein powder and skim milk

Calories - 183

Fat - .5g

Protein - 32g

Carbohydrates - 12.5g

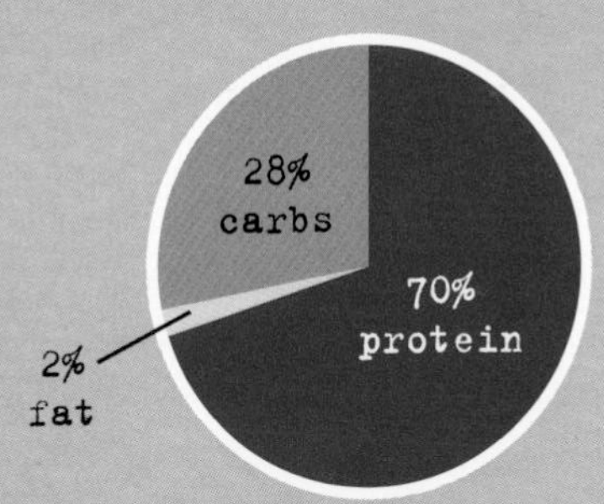

Super Purple Drink

(1 serving)

1/4 c "super" juice or orange juice
10 frozen blueberries
3 frozen strawberries
1 scoop vanilla protein powder
1/2 c water
1/4 c ice or more if you want a thicker drink

Blend well.

The "super" juice I refer to is sold in your grocery store in the refrigerated veggie section. There are several brands to choose from. They come in several types, green and purple are my favorites. My 4 year old daughter loves them too. They are packed with some extra nutrients. Apart from several juice purees there are also ingredients like green tea, spinach juice, wheat grass and garlic just to name a few. I know this sounds terrible but it tastes just like a thick juice drink. Try it you'll like it.

Other Good Ideas!

–Great for your kids as a yummy summer treat.

–Perfect to fuel a workout!

–Freeze and make a "sorbet" or a popscicle with this. YUMMY

Nutrition Per Serving

Calories - 264

Fat - 3g

Protein - 22g

Carbohydrates - 39g

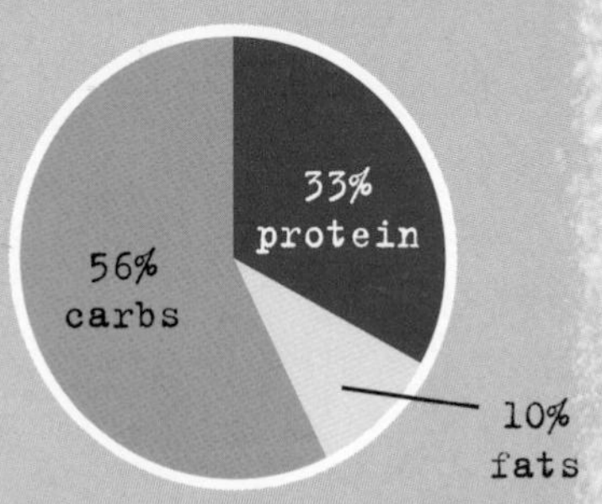

Peach Dream Shake

(1 serving)

1/2 c 1% milk or vanilla rice milk
1/2 c orange juice
6 frozen peach slices
1/2 t vanilla
1 scoop vanilla protein powder
1/4 c ice or more if you want a thicker shake

Blend well.

Other Good Ideas!

- –add blueberries, strawberries or banana to jazz it up a little
- –Perfect grab and go breakfast
- –Great for a pre or post workout energy drink

Nutrition Per Serving

Calories - 331

Fat - 4g

Protein - 27g

Carbohydrates - 50g

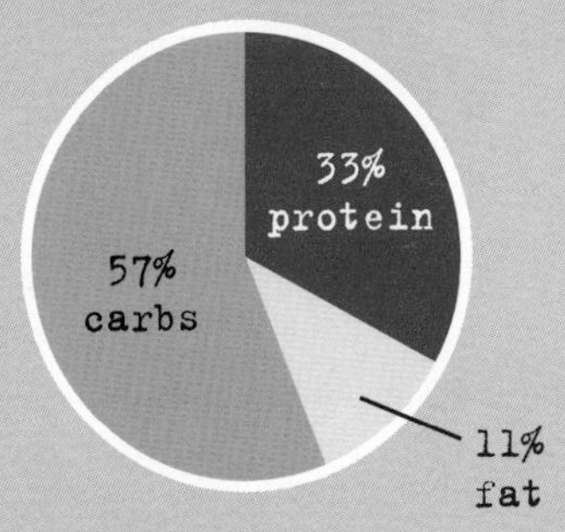

Strawberry Dream Shake

(1 serving)

1/2 c 1% milk or Vanilla rice milk
6 frozen strawberries
1 Scoop protein powder
1/2 banana
1/2 c orange juice
1/4 c ice if you want it thicker

Blend well.

My Favorite

Other Good Ideas!

- –Frozen bananas that have been pre sliced work really well for your shakes.
- –Great mid afternoon pick me up
- –Workout booster

Nutrition Per Serving

Calories - 331
Fat - 4g
Protein - 27 g
Carbohydrates - 49g

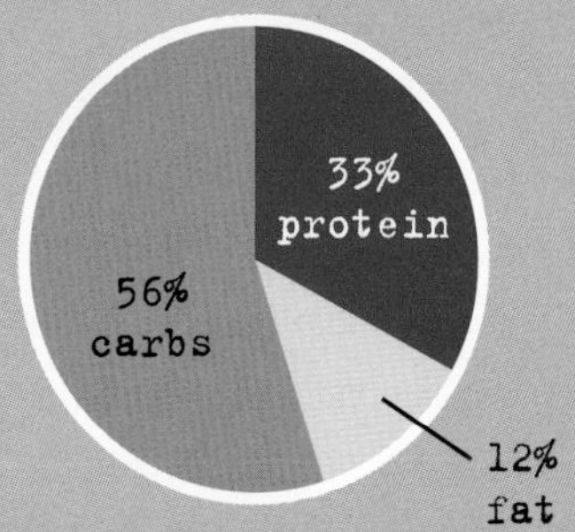

Pomegranate Vanilla Shake

(1 serving)

1/ 2 c pomegranate juice
1 scoop vanilla protein powder
1/ 2 c water
5 frozen strawberries

Blend, blend, blend. If you want to use fresh strawberries add an extra 1/2 c of ice to make the shake thicker.

Other Good Ideas!

-Pomegranate-blueberry juice works really well too

Nutrition
Per Serving

Calories - 211

Fat - 0g

Protein - 24g

Carbohydrates - 27 g

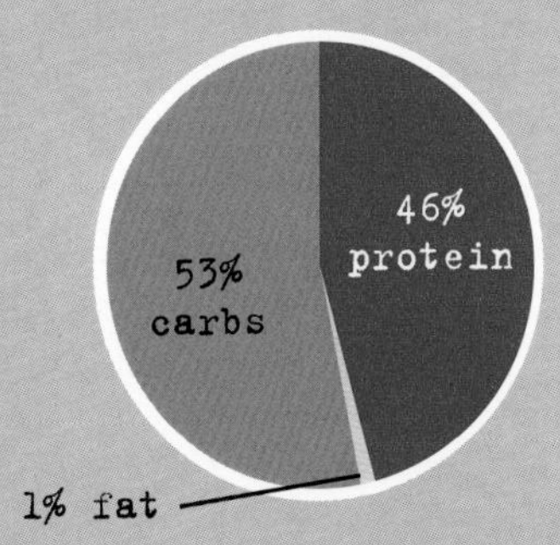

Easy and Quick things To Do With Cottage Cheese

Try Adding

- Fresh berries and honey or sweetener
- Cooked cinnamon apples
- Your favorite yogurt
- Chopped celery, pepper, celery salt
- 2 T Chocolate pudding mix or your favorite flavor
- Cocoa powder & sweetener
- A teaspoon of low sugar jam
- Chocolate protein powder
- Natural peanut butter
- Some dry ranch dip (seasoning) for an easy veggie dip
- Salsa and tuna

Just in case you were tired of just plain old cottage cheese. Try these quick ideas. I like to use a stick blender on the entire tub of cottage cheese and make it completely smooth. From there it's easy. Try blending in some natural peanut butter for a sweet treat or your favorite dry seasonings for a protein packed dip for raw veggies.

Green Chili Chipotle Dip

(4 SERVINGS)

1 pound low fat cottage cheese - blended smooth
5 T roasted garlic salsa
1 T chipotle chilis in adobo sauce (canned)
1 t cumin
1 t garlic powder
8 ounces no fat sour cream
1 t onion powder

Put all of the ingredients in a food processor or blender and blend until smooth.

Other Good Ideas!

-Great for a veggie platter

-Add a bit of vinegar to make a creamy dressing

-add to the breakfast burrito for a creamy authentic flavor

Nutrition Per Serving

Calories- 138

Fat - 1g

Protein - 16g

Carbohydrates - 14g

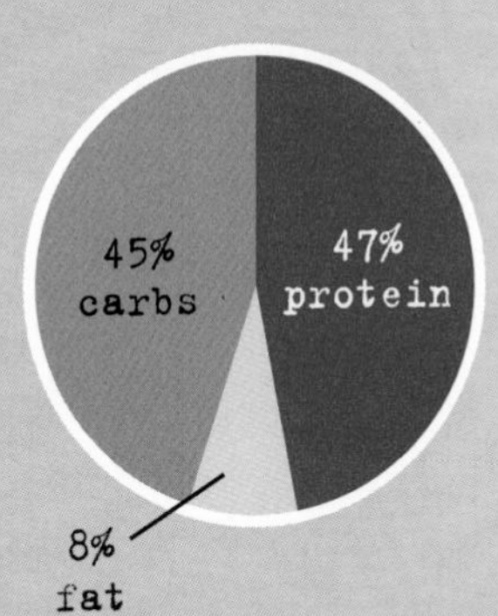

Notes:

PORK & GAME

Slow Cooked BBQ Game

(5 servings)

Venison is truly high protein yet lower calories and lower fat than most beef. If you can get it, give it a try, you just might love it.

1 T chili garlic sauce
1/2 onion sliced
2 T Catsup
1 T lime Juice
1 T spicy brown mustard
1 T cider vinegar
1 t basil
1 t garlic powder
2 pound roast *(Venison, Elk, Moose, or Beef)*

Mix all seasonings together to make a paste and pour over the meat and the onions. Let marinate overnight in the refrigerator. Start the crock pot in the morning on low and add...

1 10 oz can tomatoes with green chilis *(spicy or mild)*
salt meat lightly.

Let cook all day till it shreds easily with a fork. Excellent served over plain brown rice with a big salad on the side.

Nutrition Per Serving

using venison

Calories - 298

Fat - 6g

Protein - 55g

Carbohydrates - 7g

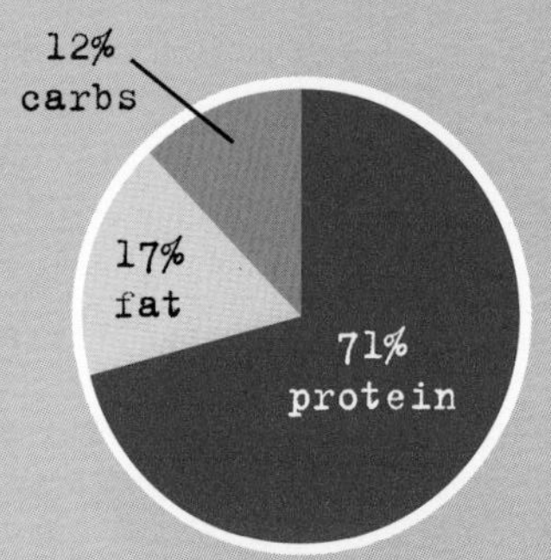

Other Good Ideas!

–Makes delicious "Sloppy Joes"

Pecan Crusted Chops

(6 servings)

---

6 center cut pork chops - 1" thick (5 oz each)
1/4 cup pecans - processed till meal *(small bits - not ground)*
1 T chili garlic paste
1 T country style or grainy mustard
1/4 t pepper
salt to taste

Trim all visible fat from chops. Spray large baking dish with non-stick spray. Lightly salt both sides of chops. Mix the rest of the ingredients in a small bowl then place this mixture on top and press in. Place in hot oven- 400 degrees- for 40 minutes or until the internal temperature of the meat is 170 degrees. Now, turn on broiler
- Broil till bubbly - 3 minutes.

Other Good Ideas!

–These are great served with a simple whole grain like bulgur or a brown rice pilaf

Nutrition Per Serving

Calories - 336
Fat - 17g
Protein - 42g
Carbohydrates - 1g

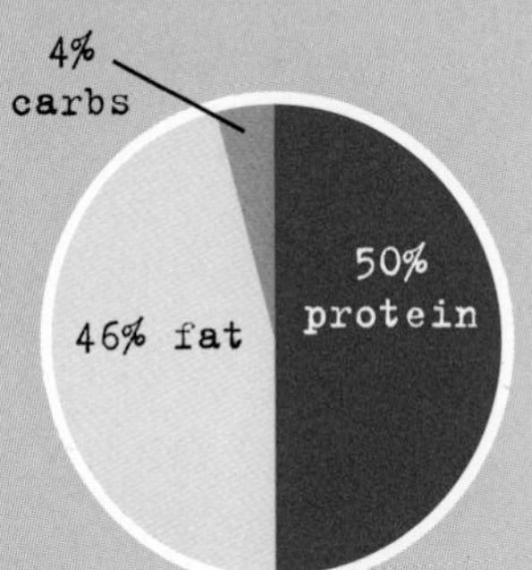

Slow Roasted Pork

(6 SERVINGS)

2 T oil
1 1/2 lbs. lean pork stew meat
1 medium onion chopped
1 sweet red pepper chopped
1/2 cup celery chopped
1/2 tsp each of salt & pepper
1 t cumin
1 t chili powder
2 t garlic powder
1 14 oz can tomatoes
2 cups broth & 1 cup water
2 T lime juice
2 sprigs fresh thyme
add some potatoes & carrots last hour if you like

Combine all ingredients in a slow cooker and mix well.
Cook on low all day.

SERVE over brown rice or quinoa.

Other Good Ideas!

- Use your leftovers to make a pulled pork sandwich
- Just add some diluted BBQ sauce or salsa
- Serve in corn tortillas with slices of avocado for a Mexican lunch

NUTRITION Per Serving

Calories - 307
Fat - 16g
Protein - 35g
Carbohydrates - 4g

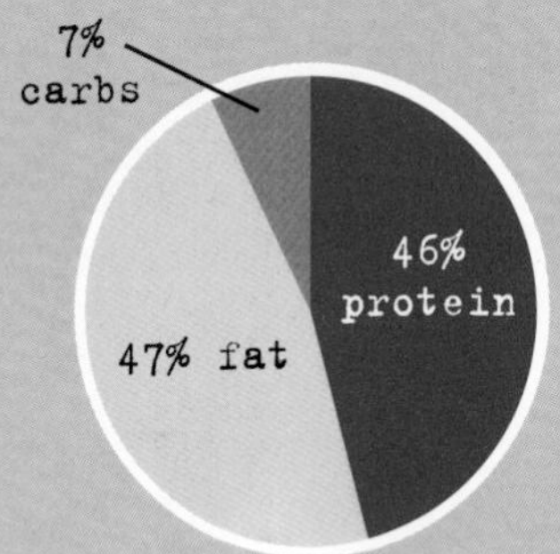

Blackened Wild Thing Burgers

(6 servings)

2 lbs. Ground "game"- *I used moose and it was great.*
2 t garlic powder
4 shakes hot sauce
6 splashes Worchestershire sauce
1 t onion powder
1/2 small onion minced
1/2 t cumin
1/2 t chili powder
1 T "blackened" seasoning

Mix everything except the last ingredient into the meat - let sit for an hour or more in the refrigerator. Remove from the refrigerator and make 6 patties and season the outside generously with "blackened seasoning". Cook on medium high heat until done. CAUTION! Don't overcook the game or it will get dry.

Other Good Ideas!

- Top with guacamole and sweet and sour onions (p.130)
- Serve on a big whole grain bun or alone with a big side of oven roasted vegetables

Venison is an amazingly high protein low fat meat. If you don't have access to any, try buffalo. It's a nice change.

Nutrition Per Serving

just burger, no toppings

Calories - 243

Fat - 5g

Protein - 46g

Carbohydrates - 1g

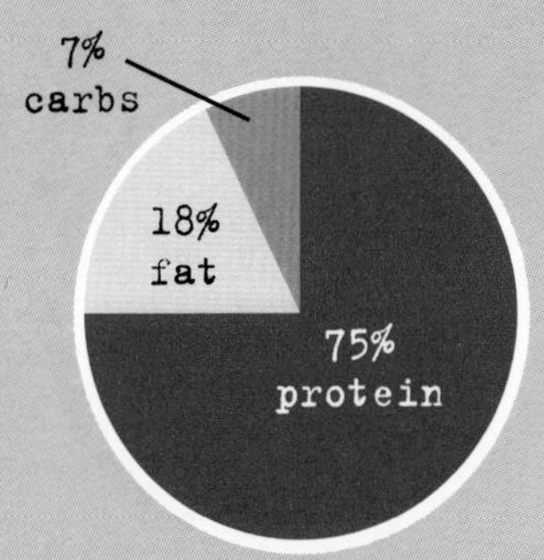

Roasted Herb Rubbed Pork Loin

(8 servings)

3 pound pork loin
marinate in-
3 T soy sauce
1 T chili garlic paste
1 t garlic powder
1 T lime juice

Refrigerate the meat for a few hours in the marinade. Remove from fridge, pat dry and coat with the dry rub.

Dry rub-
1/2 T onion powder
1 T garlic powder
1 t cumin
1 t basil
1/2 t salt and pepper
1 t paprika
dash cayenne pepper- *or more if you want heat*
1/8 t marjoram

Mix the dry rub together really well in a small bowl then apply it to the meat after removing it from the marinade. Cook in a 375 degree oven uncovered for approximately 1 hour or until the internal temperature reaches 170 degrees on a meat thermometer.

Other Good Ideas!

–the leftovers make a great sandwich with some sliced avocado and grilled onions

Nutrition Per Serving

Calories - 382
Fat - 22g
Protein - 43g
Carbohydrates - 0g

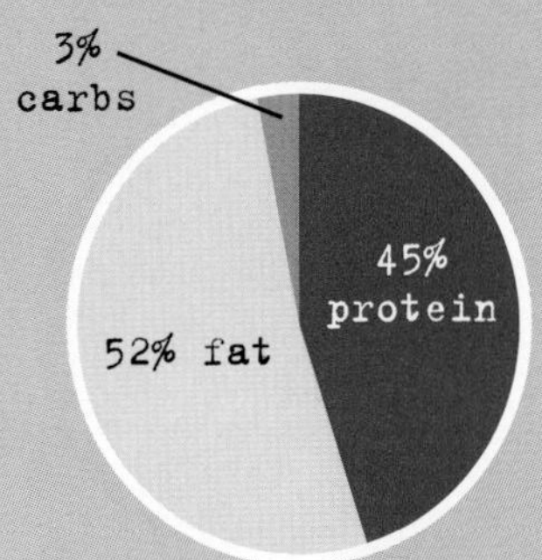

Balsamic Pork Chops

(4 servings)

4–5 ounce center cut pork chops- *all visible fat removed*
2 T balsamic vinegar
1/3 c roasted garlic salsa
3 scallions chopped
1 T olive oil
lots of pepper

Marinate the pork in the vinegar and salsa for 15 to 30 minutes. Heat the oil in a med hot skillet and quickly cook the scallions for a couple of minutes. Add the chops and cook for approximately 9-11 minutes on each side until any liquid is reduced and the chops are browned on both sides and cooked through the center.

Other Good Ideas!

–These are really good on the grill

–Try grilling some sliced zucchini, eggplant and onions to go along with the pork

These are your every day easy and go with everything pork chops.

Nutrition Per Serving

Calories - 345
Fat - 18g
Protein - 42g
Carbohydrates - 2g

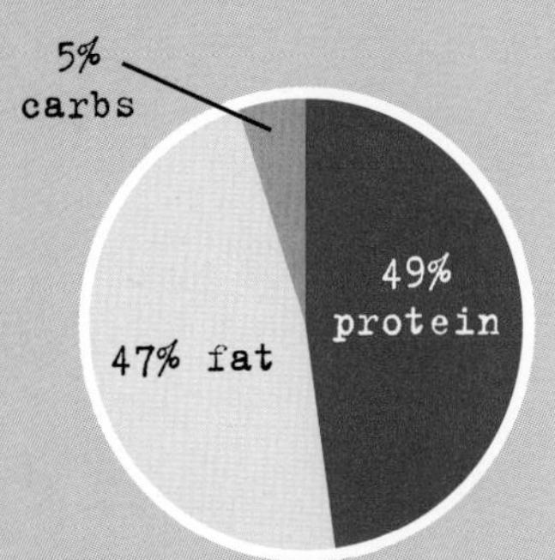

NOTES:

GRAINS

Moe's Kid Tested Granola Bars

(12 servings)

THESE ARE EASY AND THE KIDS LOVE THEM. GREAT FOR SCHOOL SNACKS OR FOR THOSE LONG FIELD TRIPS.

1 c honey
1 c natural peanut butter
1 c rolled oats
1/2 c protein powder
1/2 c raisins
you can add other dried fruit, nuts, seeds etc.

Boil honey for about 3 minutes then add the natural peanut butter and stir well. Next add the oats, protein powder and raisins. Press mixture into a pan and let cool. Cut into bars and wrap individually for an easy travel meal.

Nutrition Per Serving

Calories - 268

Fat - 11g

Protein - 8g

Carbohydrates - 38g

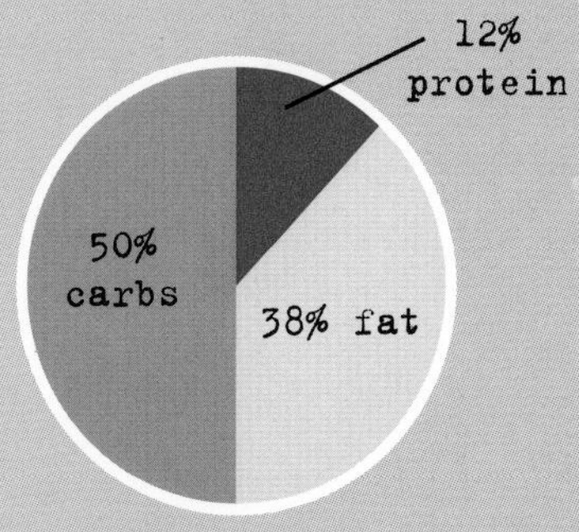

Honey Kissed Granola

(12 servings)

---

non-stick oil spray
2 cups old-fashioned oats
1/3 cup slivered almonds
1/3 cup flaked unsweetened coconut
1/3 cup chopped nuts *(pecans, cashews, walnuts, sunflower seeds)*
1/3 cup fruit juice *(apple, orange, cranberry…)*
1/3 cup honey
2 tablespoons vegetable oil
2 teaspoons ground cinnamon
1/2 teaspoon ground allspice
1 cup dried cranberries

Preheat oven to 325°F. Spray rimmed baking sheet with non-stick spray. Combine oats, almonds, coconut and nuts in large bowl. Combine juice , honey, oil, cinnamon and allspice in bowl, whisking until honey dissolves. Pour syrup over oat mixture; stir to coat evenly. Spread mixture out on prepared baking sheet. Bake until golden brown at edges, about 20 minutes. Add cranberries; use metal spatula to blend. Bake until granola is golden and beginning to dry, stirring occasionally, about 12 minutes longer. Cool completely on baking sheet.

Other Good Ideas!

- –On vanilla yogurt with protein powder
- –With skim milk
- –Put this in a pretty jar with a ribbon and give as a gift.
- –As a topping for baked cinnamon apples, mashed sweet potatoes or grilled peaches

Homemade granola is sooo GOOD!

Nutrition Per Serving

Calories - 181
Fat - 8.5g
Protein - 3g
Carbohydrates - 26g

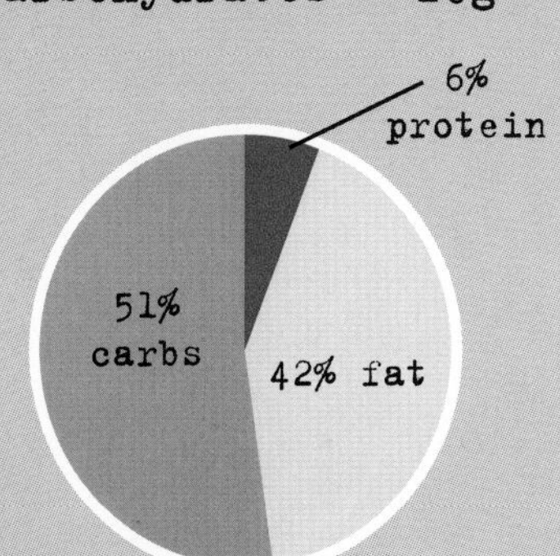

Pumpkin Pancakes
With Coconut, Cinnamon Apples

(4 servings)

---

2 c. old fashioned oats -

- *Put into food processor to make smaller but not till texture of flour.*

4 eggs
8 whites
1 c pumpkin puree
2 t cinnamon
1/2 t nutmeg
1/2 c vanilla rice milk or skim milk
1 t vanilla

Combine all ingredients and blend well. Heat a large non-stick skillet to med heat, cover pan with non-stick oil spray and add1/4 of the batter. Spread the batter out with the back of a spoon if it's thick. Cook pan cake on both sides until golden brown. Cook all of the cakes. While the cakes cook make the topping.

---

2 apples cored and thinly sliced
3 T honey
2 T shredded coconut
1 t cinnamon

Mix all together and cook in microwave for 2-3 minutes. Use as the syrup for the pancakes. You can also add a little maple syrup or sugar free syrup.

Makes enough pankakes to have a couple of great portable meals.

Nutrition
Per Serving

made with skim milk
Calories - 388
Fat - 10g
Protein - 20g
Carbohydrates - 58g

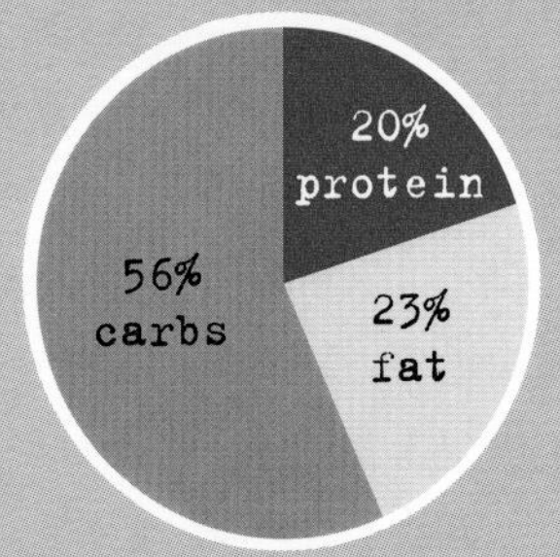

Zucchini Apple Muffins

(2 servings)

1 c oat flour *– just run whole oats through the blender or food processor*
1/2 c old fashioned oats
1 egg
5 egg whites
3/4 c shredded zucchini
1/2 c applesauce
1/2 t allspice
2 t baking powder
1 t vanilla
1 t cinnamon
2 T honey
pinch salt
1 t lemon zest

Mix everything together really well and let sit a few minutes. Spray your muffin pan with non-stick spray and fill the cups about 2/3 of the way full. Bake in a pre-heated 350 degree oven for about 25-30 minutes or until a toothpick inserted in center comes out clean.

Other Good Ideas!

–Add dried cranberries
–Add 1/2 c pureed pumpkin
–Add pecans or walnuts

These are moist and so tasty. This is an easy way to get my daughter to eat her veggies.

Nutrition Per Serving

Calories - 417
Fat - 7g
Protein - 18g
Carbohydrates - 73g

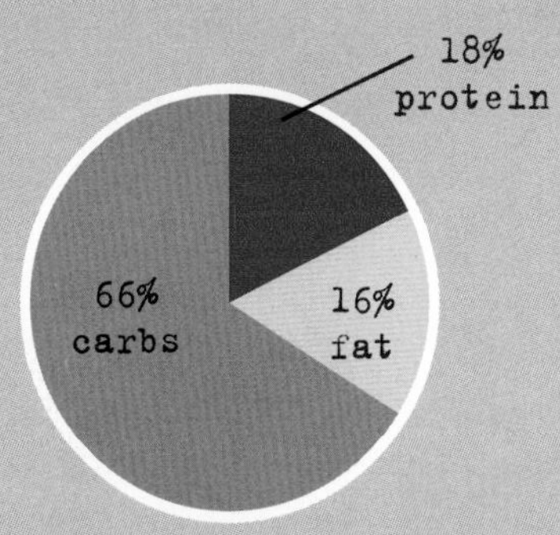

Slivered Almonds, Pecans with Cranberry & Coconut

(8 servings)

2 cups oats
1/3 cup slivered almonds
1/3 cup coconut
1/3 cup pecans
1/3 cup orange juice
1/3 cup honey
2 T oil
1 t cinnamon
1/2 t allspice
1 t vanilla
1 cup dried cranberries

Heat and mix the orange juice and honey then add the vanilla. Mix with all remaining ingredients-except the cranberries. Place in foil lined or sprayed pan. Bake in pre-heated 325° oven for 20 minutes. Add cranberries, stir, cook to dry 12 minutes.

Other Good Ideas!

–Party food

–Topping for yogurt

Nutrition Per Serving

Calories - 332

Fat - 18g

Protein - 5g

Carbohydrates - 40g

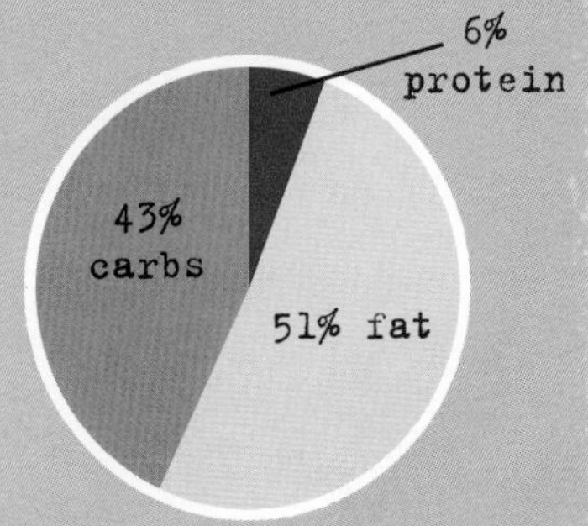

Easy Things to do with Oats

- honey and cinnamon
- apples and cinnamon *(add before cooking) with 1 t. honey*
- add 1 t peanut butter
- toasted nuts and dried cranberries
- teaspoon jelly
- applesauce and cinnamon
- maple syrup
- dried fruit such as cranberries, apricots and raisins
- mashed banana *(add before cooking)*
- chocolate protein powder and 1 t cocoa powder or peanut butter
- diced apple *(add before cooking)* with 1 t natural peanut butter

I cook my old fashioned oats every morning in the microwave. If you want to use the stove top or you are making many servings just follow the directions on the package. There is no reason to use the quick cook oats when this is so fast and tastes so much better.

In the microwave: Use a medium size microwave proof bowl (not small or it will overflow and make a sticky mess). Add your serving size of oats and cover with water plus a little more. Put a paper towel or plate under the bowl while cooking in case it does overflow. Cook for approximately 2 1/2 minutes for tender chewy oats.

Cooking Grains

Time to cook		
1 c dry - Grain	Water	Cook time
Quinoa (rinse well)	2c	20 min
Barley – pearled	2 1/2 c	40 min
Barley – whole	3 c	60 min
Brown Rice – medium grained	2 c	50 min
Brown Rice – short grained	2 c	60 min

When cooking on the stovetop, bring your water to a boil first before adding your grain. After adding the grain put the lid on, reduce heat a little, then let the grain soak up all the liquid.

Mom's Mexican Rice

(3 servings)

1 cup uncooked brown rice
1 small onion chopped
1 can tomatoes with chilis, *drain but keep liquid*
1 t garlic chopped
2 T olive oil
2 cups liquid total *- juice from tomatoes and*
1 1/2 c chicken broth
1 t cumin
1 t chili powder

Heat olive oil on medium in a large skillet with a lid. Add the onion and garlic and sauté for 5 minutes. Add the rice and cook, stirring occasionally for 10 minutes. Next, add the remainder of the ingredients, bring to a boil, reduce heat to a simmer, cover and cook for approximately 45 minutes or until the rice is tender. Add more broth if the mix gets too dry before the rice is cooked.

Other Good Ideas!

–Mix with left over chicken for a yummy meal!

–This goes with any great Tex-Mex food

Nutrition Per Serving

Calories - 258

Fat - 8g

Protein - 4g

Carbohydrates - 41g

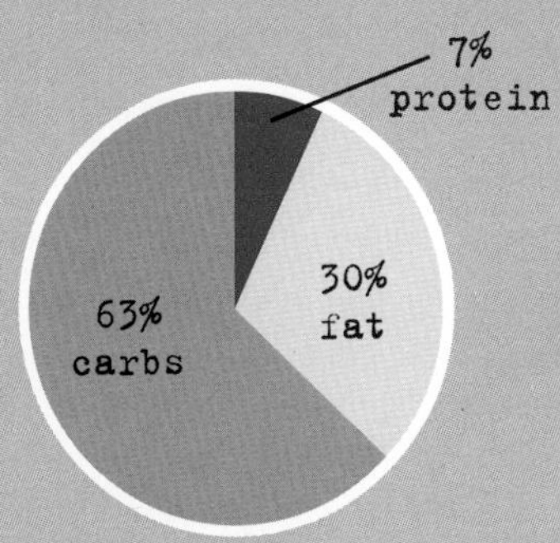

Confetti Barley

(4 servings)

1 T olive oil - flavored *(rosemary garlic is really good)* or natural
1/2 onion - chopped
15 cherry tomatoes - halved
1/2 t garlic powder
1/2 yellow pepper - chopped
salt & pepper to taste
1/2 small jalapeno - diced

Heat olive oil in skillet then cook all together in skillet on low for approximately 10 minutes. Then add:

2 cups cooked barley
1 T chopped green chilis (canned is great)
1/2 cup chicken stock
1/2 T lemon juice

Serve with grated fresh parmesan

Other Good Ideas!

–Add diced grilled chicken or pork loin for a great meal

–Chill and use as a salad for a picnic

Nutrition Per Serving

Calories - 231

Fat - 2g

Protein - 5g

Carbohydrates - 50g

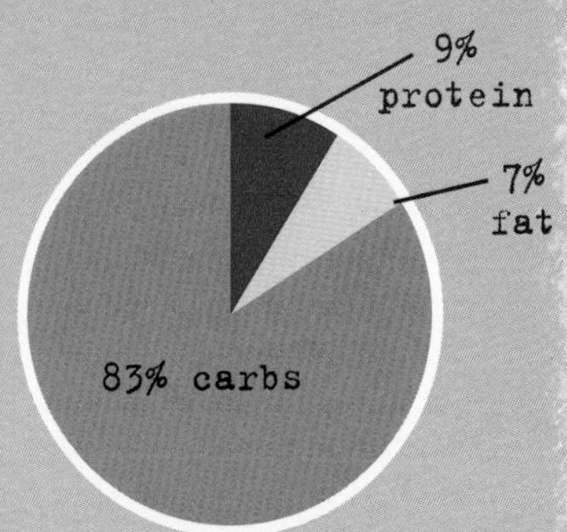

Barley Salad
With Roasted Red Peppers

(2 servings)

1 c corn
1/4 c roasted red peppers - chopped
6 scallions – bottom 4 inches chopped
1 orange sweet pepper - chopped
1/4 c fresh cilantro – chopped
1 c cooked barley
1/2 t garlic powder
2 T olive oil
2 T fresh lime or lemon juice
salt and pepper to taste

Combine all of the ingredients and mix well seasoning to taste. Chill and then serve over a big bed of greens.

Other Good Ideas!

–Add a serving of chopped chicken, canned tuna, canned salmon, shrimp.... It's all good

–If you want less oil, replace it with vinegar or plain yogurt and some sweetener to counter the tartness

Barley is excellent in salads.

It remains slightly chewy and adds bite to crunchy veggies.

Nutrition Per Serving

Calories - 300
Fat - 15g
Protein - 4g
Carbohydrates - 40g

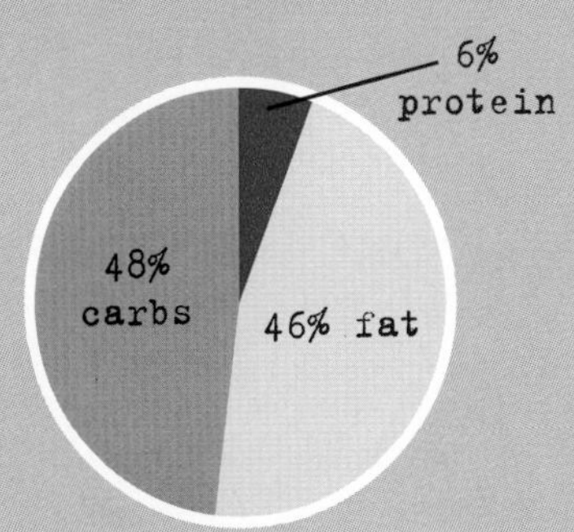

Lemon Quinoa With Asparagus Salad

(4 SERVINGS)

2 c cooked quinoa cooled
1/4 c diced onion or scallions
2 celery ribs diced
3/4 c cooked asparagus
1/2 t garlic powder
1/2 t dried dill
juice from 1 lemon
salt and pepper to taste

Just add everything to a bowl and mix well. This is great warmed as well. Serve on a pile of mixed greens.

THIS IS A SUPER SQUEAKY CARBOHYDRATE AND VEGGIE COMBO WITH AMAZING FRESH FLAVOR.

Other Good Ideas!

–Excellent served warm with roasted turkey or chicken.

NUTRITION Per Serving

Calories - 160

Fat - 2g

Protein - 5g

Carbohydrates - 29g

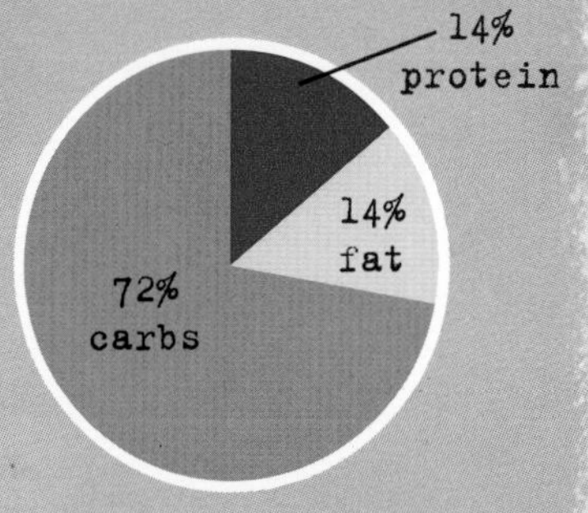

Quinoa With Caramelized Onions

(3 servings)

2 c cooked quinoa
1/2 of a sweet onion thinly sliced
1 T olive oil
2 pinches pepper
1 pinch red pepper flakes or more if you like it spicy
2 T soy sauce
1/2 t honey

Heat the oil in a small sauce pan on medium heat. Add the onion and cook for a couple of minutes. Turn heat down and add all of the ingredients except the quinoa. You will have to stir often or the onions will burn. Cook for about 10 minutes until the onions are really well done and soft. Turn off the heat and add the quinoa. Mix well and let the quinoa warm up before serving.

Serve warm or cold.

Other Good Ideas!

- I like this best with roast beef or steak since the flavors are so rich
- Excellent cold leftovers

This is one of my favorite recipes in the whole book and it's so simple.

Nutrition Per Serving

Calories - 160
Fat - 3g
Protein - 5g
Carbohydrates - 30g

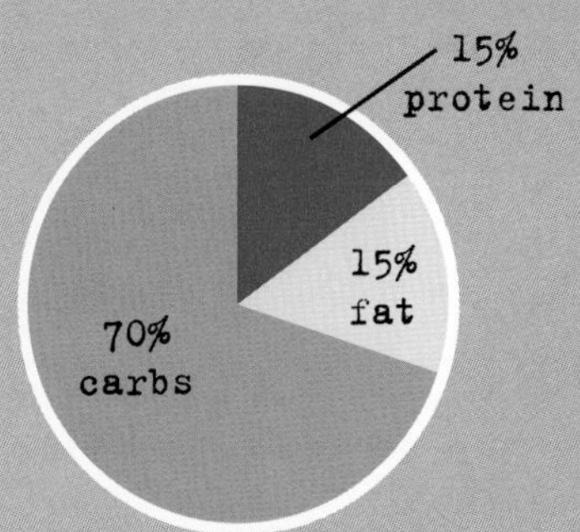

Easy Quinoa Salmon Salad

(3 servings)

3 c cooked quinoa
1 red sweet pepper-diced
1 cucumber-diced
1 bunch scallions-chopped
1 medium zucchini-chopped
1 14oz can Pink Salmon drained well and rinsed

Simple, elegant and yummy.

Dressing

juice of 1 lemon
3 T fresh dill
2 T balsamic vinegar
3 T olive oil
1 T garlic powder

Mix the quinoa, salmon and the veggies together in a medium bowl. In a small bowl add all of the liquids and seasonings and whisk well. Pour the dressing over the salad. Serve immediately or chill.

Other Good Ideas!

- Very portable meal all in one container
- To make this really special, grill some fresh salmon or tuna with olive oil and lemon juice to flake into the salad

Nutrition Per Serving

Calories - 610
Fat - 13g
Protein - 43g
Carbohydrates - 78g

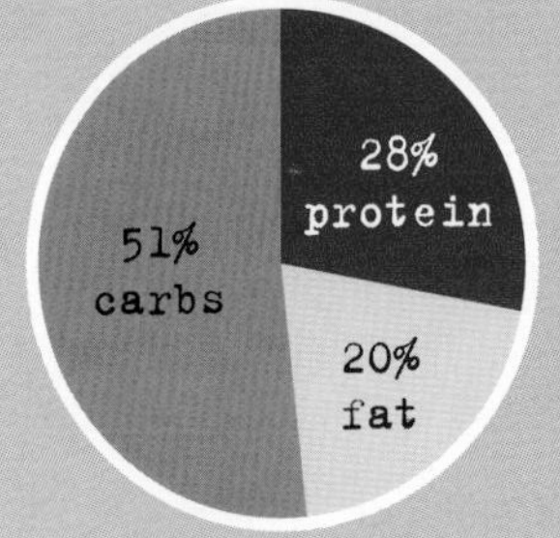

Quinoa & Wild Rice

by Lynne Anderson

ISSA certified PT

(8 servings)

1 c wild rice
1 c quinoa
2 onions chopped
1 1/2 c sliced mushrooms
1 red bell pepper chopped
1 yellow bell pepper chopped
2 T olive oil
4 c no fat chicken stock

Cook wild rice in chicken stock for 45 minutes adding water if necessary to keep from drying out. While rice is cooking, heat oil in large skillet. Add veggies, starting with the peppers and onions. Cook 3 minutes then add the mushrooms and cook until tender. When the rice is finished, add the quinoa to the rice along with some water if needed. Cook 15-20 minutes more until the quinoa is soft.

Spray a large casserole dish with no stick spray. Mix the veggies and rice mixture together and turn into the casserole dish. Bake at 350 degrees for 15 minutes. You can also stir in some sauteed chicken breast or cooked ground beef to make a complete meal.

Great for holiday meals

Other Good Ideas!

–Take to a potluck dinner

–Really good with turkey or chicken – think holidays

Nutrition Per Serving

Calories - 245
Fat - 9g
Protein - 8g
Carbohydrates - 34g

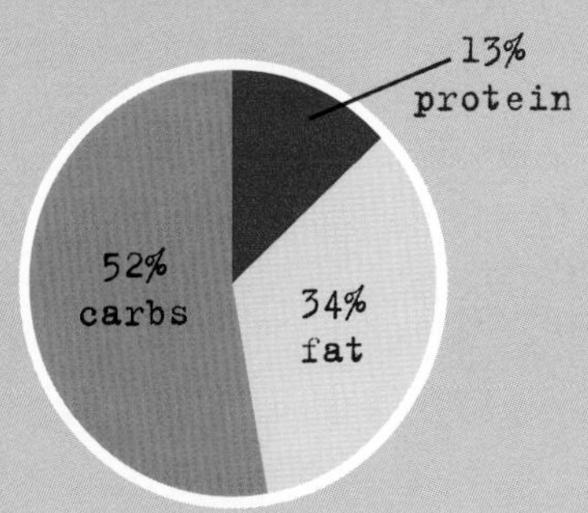

Notes:

POTATOES

Sweet Potato Breakfast Cakes

(4 servings)

1 1/2 cups mashed cooked sweet potatoes
1 egg
1 t vanilla
dash salt
1/2 t cinnamon
1 T honey
1/2 cups oat flour *– grind your own in a food processor*
1 T canola oil

Mix everything together except for the oil. Let mixture sit for 10 minutes. Heat oil in non-stick pan on medium heat. When hot, roll the potato mixture into 8 balls and flatten. Cook until slightly browned on each side. This takes a few minutes per side. The cakes should be cooked through but soft on the inside and crispy and brown on the outside.

A new twist on an old favorite.

Other Good Ideas!

–Top with a bit of real maple syrup or some vanilla yogurt with toasted almonds on top

–Serve with some cooked cinnamon apples spooned over the top

Nutrition Per Serving

Calories - 188
Fat - 6 g
Protein - 5g
Carbohydrates - 30g

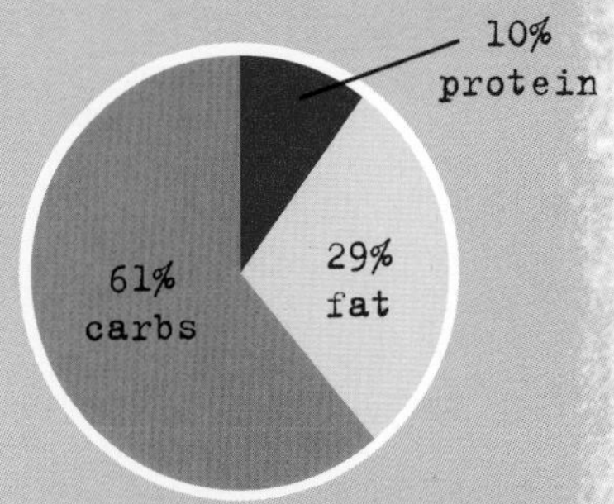

Stuffed Baby Taters

(5 servings)

10 smallish (1.5-2 inches long) gold potatoes
salt and pepper to taste
3 cloves garlic – minced
5 scallions – minced
1/2 c lowfat (or fat free)sour cream
3 T shredded Parmesan cheese *(or your favorite cheese)*
2-3 shakes paprika

Boil the small gold potatoes till tender. Drain and let cool until you can handle them. Pre-heat oven to 350 degrees.

Trim off the bottom of each potato so each will sit upright in a baking dish. Put the trimmed parts in a bowl and now do the same for the tops. Use a fruit baller or something small and sharp to scoop out part of the center of each tater.

For the filling, puree the tater trimmings, salt and pepper, scallions, garlic, and sour cream. Stuff the little taters and sprinkle some of your favorite cheese on top plus some paprika. Bake in oven for 10 minutes at 350 degrees to heat up and melt the cheese.

Other Good Ideas!

–Excellent Party food

–Be creative, if it goes with a potato try stuffing it inside, try turkey sausage, cream cheese, sage, butter….

If you love a twice baked potato, try this one.

Nutrition Per Serving

Calories - 191
Fat - 4g
Protein - 5g
Carbohydrates - 35g

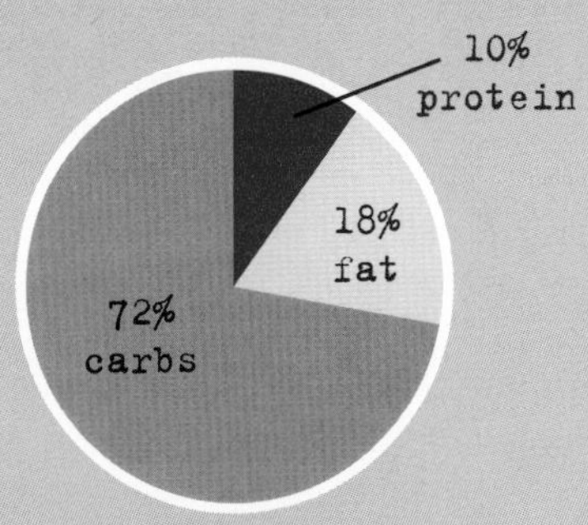

Savory Sweet Potatoes

(Approximately 4 servings)

Spicy, sweet, and savory all rolled into one simple, healthy dish.

2 medium sweet potatoes peeled and cut into 1/2" cubes
2 T olive oil
pinch cumin
pinch ground ginger
pinch salt
pinch pepper
pinch paprika
juice from 1 lime

Heat non-stick skillet with the oil on med heat, cook approximately 15 minutes then turn the heat up to medium high and cook until golden brown and a little crispy. Stir often. They will burn easily once they start cooking. Squirt fresh lime juice on the sweet potatoes just before serving (optional step).

Other Good Ideas!

- –Great cooked in the oven too
- –Excellent side for turkey and chicken
- –If you want less fat – use a nonstick skillet with just a tsp of oil

Nutrition Per Serving

Calories - 121

Fat - 7g

Protein - 1g

Carbohydrates - 14g

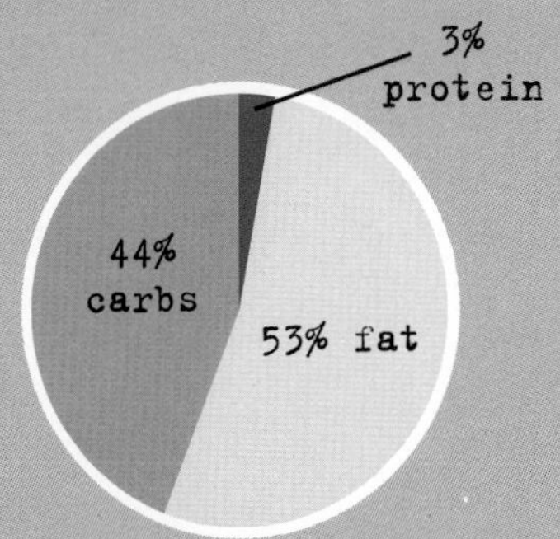

Sweet Potato Fries

(4 servings)

2 medium sweet potatoes *-peeled and cut into thick fries*
1 T olive oil
1 T creole seasoning

Preheat oven to 350 degrees. Put fries and oil into a large bowl and really try to coat the potatoes well. Add more oil if you like. Spread the fries in a single layer on a foil or parchment covered sheet pan sprayed with non-stick spray. Sprinkle the fries with the seasoning. Be generous it's really tasty.

Cook for approximately 15 minutes then flip the fries and cook for another15-20 minutes until they start to brown and are fork tender and browned on the outside.

Other Good Ideas!

-Try some other seasonings… cinnamon and ginger, seasoned salt and garlic powder, lemon pepper or chinese five spice. There are lots of great combinations

-Take to a party with some cool guacamole dip or most any dip. It's a nice change from veggie sticks

Some people are always surprised when I serve sweet potatoes and it's not a holiday. Try them they are a wonderful starchy vegetable and a nice change.

Nutrition Per Serving

Calories - 90
Fat - 3.5g
Protein - 1g
Carbohydrates - 14g

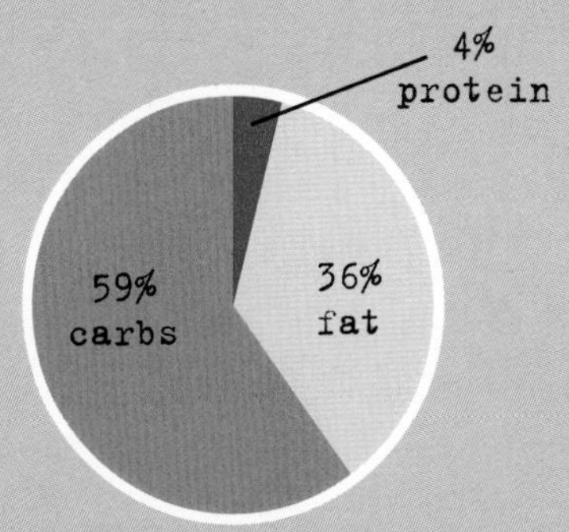

Warm Potato Salad

(4 servings)

Awesome picnic food.

2 slices turkey bacon chopped into small pieces
3 T olive oil
4 T cider vinegar
1/2 t Succunat or sugar *(Succunat is a raw unprocessed sugar)*
1 t garlic powder
salt and pepper to taste
2 T roasted red peppers (from a jar, drained) minced
3 c cooked red potatoes, cubed
1/2 diced celery
4 scallions sliced

While the potatoes are cooking, cook the bacon until browned in a non-stick skillet. After it's finished turn the heat off. Let it cool for a couple of minutes then add the oil, vinegar, sweetener, and seasonings to the pan. Combine everything well and let sit. In a bowl, combine the rest of the ingredients then add the dressing and toss together.

Serve warm.

Other Good Ideas!

–This is also great cold with chopped grilled chicken as a salad.

Nutrition Per Serving

Calories - 206

Fat - 11g

Protein - 3.5g

Carbohydrates - 24g

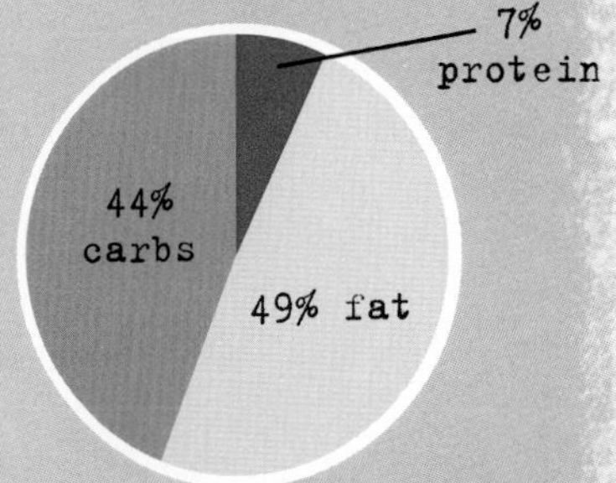

Pan Fried Sweet Taters

(4 servings)

---

2 medium sweet potatoes
1 t cumin
1 t garlic powder
1/4 t cayenne – or more if ya like it hot
2 t olive oil
salt and pepper to taste

Peel and slice the taters into 1/8" rounds. Heat the skillet to medium heat, add 1 t oil and put in a single layer of taters with a little overlap. Flip when the first side starts to brown, this takes several minutes. Mix dry ingredients in a small bowl. When the taters are soft and browned a little on both sides slide them onto a plate and sprinkle with the seasoning mix. Keep it up until they are all cooked. Serve next to your favorite burger.

Sort of like sweet chips

Nutrition Per Serving

Calories - 121
Fat - 7g
Protein - 1g
Carbohydrates - 14g

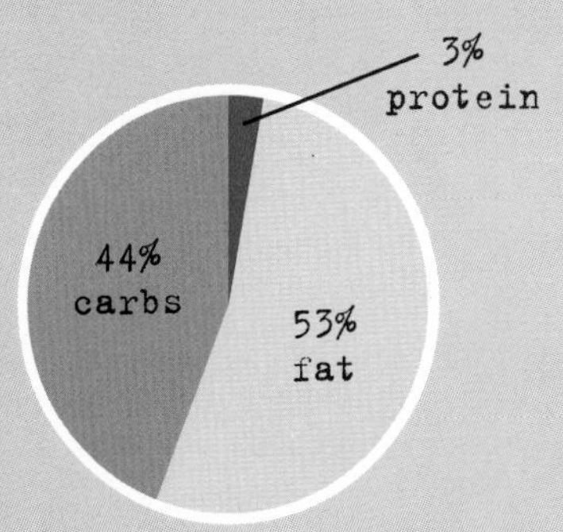

NOTES:

VEGETABLES

Rosemary Roasted Vegetables

(5 servings)

1/2 carton button mushrooms- *trimmed & cleaned (approximately 20)*

2 small zucchini cut into 1.5 inch chunks
1 yellow squash cut into same size chunks
1 large red pepper cut into 1 inch wide strips

Marinate vegetables for a couple hours at room temp in

---

2 T flavored olive oil or plain olive oil *(rosemary garlic is great)*
2 t garlic powder
2 T balsamic vinegar
2 t chopped fresh rosemary

Toss everything into a baggie or bowl and stir or turn a few times while marinating.

Preheat oven to 400 degrees and cook veggies in a shallow dish for 20-30 minutes or until zucchini is tender.

Other Good Ideas!

- These vegetables are just as good the next day as part of a salad with a serving of brown rice, grilled chicken and a great vinaigrette dressing
- Marinate ahead of time in a tightly sealed container for a more intense flavor

Nutrition Per Serving

Calories - 115

Fat - 10g

Protein - 3g

Carbohydrates - 5g

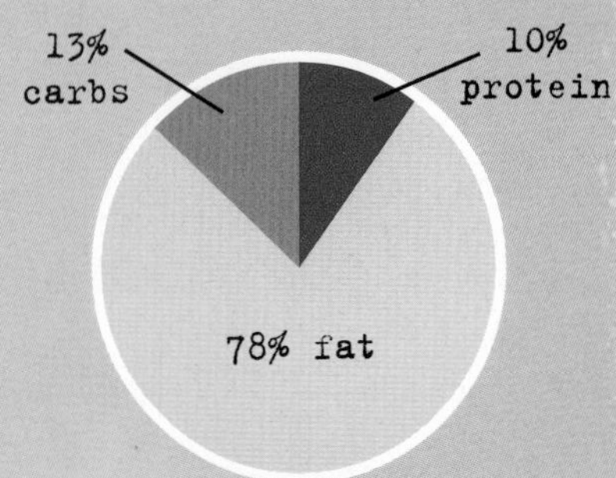

Marinated Carrots & Peppers

(4 servings)

3 cups carrots chopped
1 red sweet pepper chopped to same size as carrots

Dressing

1 jalapeno minced
1/2 T mustard - spicy brown or Dijon
1 T chili garlic sauce
1 T honey
1 lime juiced and
1/4 t of lime zest
3/4 cup cider vinegar

Mix & heat dressing in microwave for 30 or so seconds to melt honey. Mix well and pour on veggies. Salt & pepper to taste. Refrigerate and stir every so often. Careful… the heat intensifies with refrigeration time.

Other Good Ideas!

- Side salad with fajitas
- Use to top a turkey avocado sandwich
- Top any salad

This is a spicy pickled veggie dish.

Try some other veggies WOW!

Nutrition Per Serving

Calories - 67
Fat - .5 g
Protein - 1g
Carbohydrates - 17g

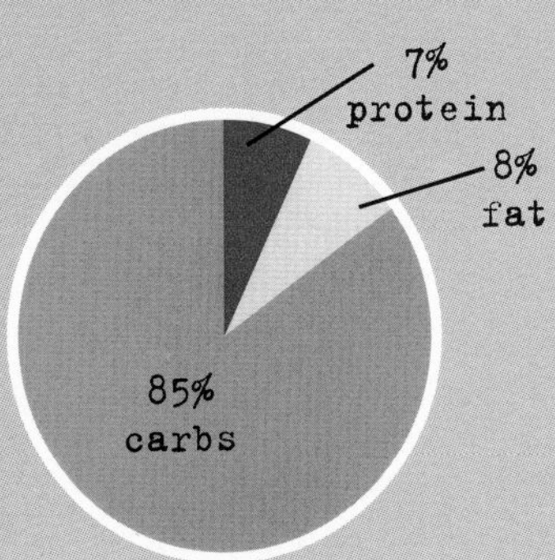

Simply Spaghetti Squash

(5 servings)

1 whole spaghetti squash

Cut squash in half - scoop out seeds - place in glass pie plate cut side down, add 1/2" water. Microwave for 10 minutes covered with plastic wrap. Remove from microwave and hold onto the squash with one fork and shred the squash with another fork. Salt & pepper to taste. Now add the following to the squash.

2 T butter or olive oil
2 T grated parmesan cheese

Put the butter and cheese on the shredded squash and let melt. Mix well.

Have you tried this vegetable? Please do. The flavor is very mild and kids think it's pasta.

Other Good Ideas!

–Top with spaghetti sauce- who knew?

Nutrition Per Serving

made with butter - 1 cup

Calories - 82

Fat - 4g

Protein - 3g

Carbohydrates - 11g

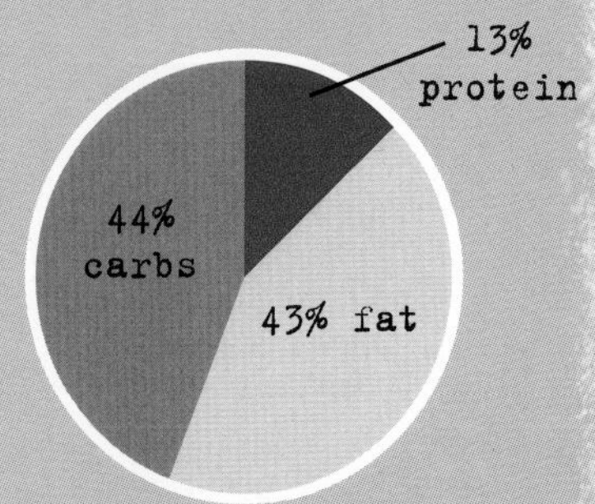

Sesame Broccoli

(5 servings)

5 cups chopped broccoli steamed
until fork tender

Drain off water.
Then add...

1 T sesame seeds
5 drops toasted sesame oil

Toss together – salt and pepper to taste

Other Good Ideas!

–This recipe is great with sugar snap peas and also asparagus instead of broccoli

Fast

Easy

Delicious

Nutrition Per Serving

Calories - 34

Fat - 1g

Protein - 3g

Carbohydrates - 5g

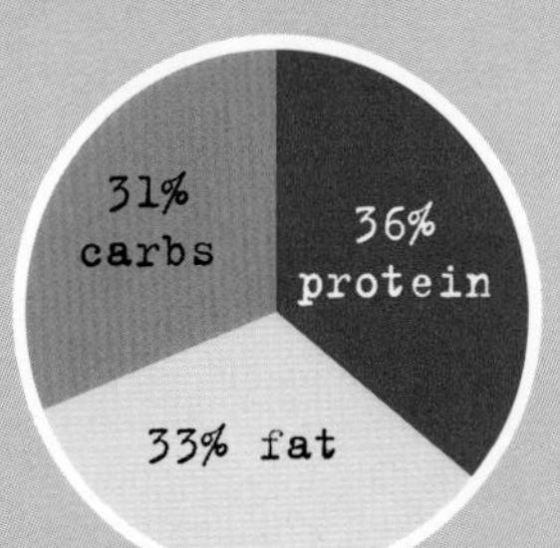

Corn Tomato Salsa

(4-5 servings)

14 oz can tomatoes-drained
4 oz can green chilis-drained
8 oz can corn, drained
1 avocado diced small
small bunch of scallions-chopped whites only
1 T red wine vinegar
juice from 1 lime
1 t garlic powder
salt and pepper to taste

Mix all ingredients well. Serve or refrigerate.

Fresh

&

Simple!

Other Good Ideas!

- –Good side dish with any grilled meat
- –Enjoy solo as a salad or just add chicken or tuna for a meal
- –Use as a spread for a chicken sandwich

Nutrition Per Serving

Calories - 114

Fat - 7g

Protein - 3g

Carbohydrates - 15g

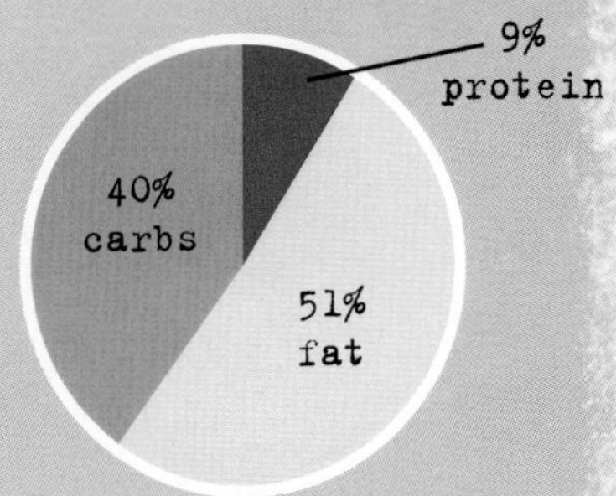

Stuffed Mushrooms

(5 servings)

10 large button mushrooms *-approximately 2 inches across*
1 T olive oil
hot sauce to taste (5-6 dashes is a good start)
1/2 t garlic powder
1 T Worcestershire sauce
3 oz turkey breakfast sausage, bulk style
1 bunch scallions chopped small
3 T lite cream cheese
1/4 t sage
salt and pepper
3 T parmesan cheese

Clean the mushrooms and remove the stems at the base of the cap. Run all of the stems through the food processor or chop until very small. Sautee the sausage and scallions on med heat until the sausage is cooked, approximately 5-10 minutes. Add remaining ingredients and cook another 5 minutes. Pre-Heat oven to 425 Degrees, mix everything together well and spoon into the mushroom caps. Top mixture with a sprinkling of parmesan cheese. Cook in a baking dish in a 425 degree oven for 10 minutes or until heated thoroughly.

Healthy Party Food.

Other Good Ideas!

-Great party food
-Elegant side dish at holiday meals

Nutrition Per Serving

Calories - 115
Fat - 9g
Protein - 8g
Carbohydrates - 3g

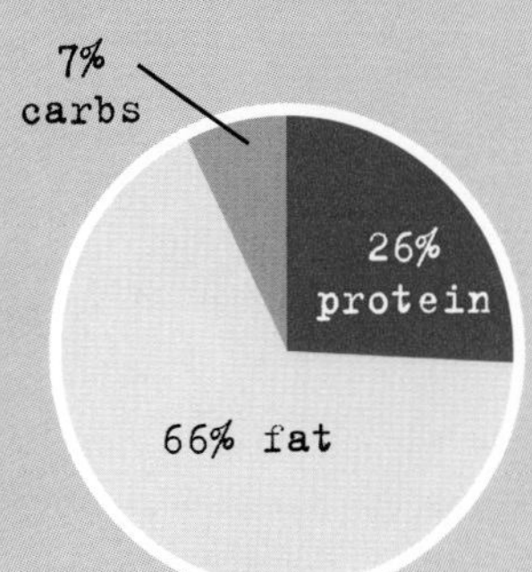

Saucy Spaghetti Squash

(4 servings)

4 c cooked spaghetti squash
1 T olive oil
2 crushed garlic cloves
1/2 c yellow onion diced
1/2 c pureed cooked great northern beans or cooked lentils
1/4 t marjoram
1/4 t basil
1/4 t oregano
1-15 oz can "no salt" diced tomatoes with the juice
salt and pepper

Cut squash in half - scoop out seeds - place in glass pie plate with the cut side down - add 1/2 inch of water to the dish. Microwave on high for 10 minutes covered with plastic wrap. Hold onto the squash with one fork and shred the squash with another fork.

Heat a large non-stick skillet then add oil, onion and garlic and cook on medium heat until the onion starts to soften. Stir occasionally. Now add in all of the seasonings, the tomatoes and the puree and simmer for about 15 minutes. Stir in the spaghetti squash and let it simmer long enough to reheat. Salt and pepper to taste.

Voila!

Lower

carbohydrate

and

low fat.

Other Good Ideas!

–Add other veggies to the sauce like zucchini and red peppers

–Serve with a thinly sliced chicken breast on top.

Nutrition Per Serving

Calories - 141

Fat - 4g

Protein - 4g

Carbohydrates - 24g

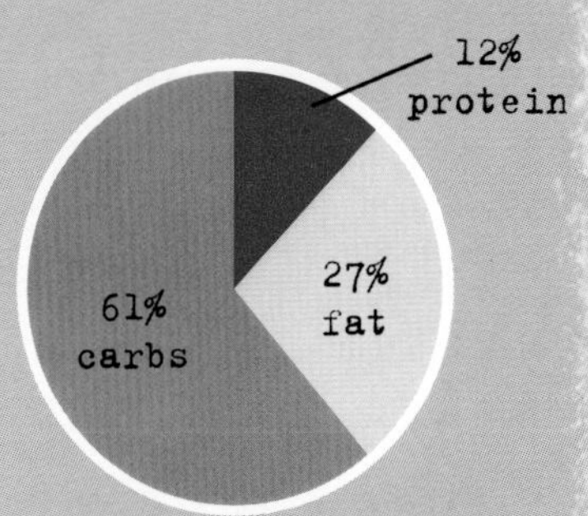

Sauteed Green Cabbage

(4 servings)

1 head green cabbage thinly sliced
1 T olive oil
1 clove minced garlic

Heat the oil in a large skillet and then add the garlic. Let cook for a few seconds to flavor the oil a little bit, stir a few times so it won't burn. Add the cabbage, pile it on. It will reduce in size by about 3/4 so just try to keep it in the pan at the beginning. Use tongs and stir the cabbage until it is all evenly cooked.

Fast and Easy!

Other Good Ideas!

- This is great served with pork loin or roast beef.
- Slice an onion and sauté a little first before you add the cabbage.

Nutrition Per Serving

Calories - 85
Fat - 4g
Protein - 3g
Carbohydrates - 12g

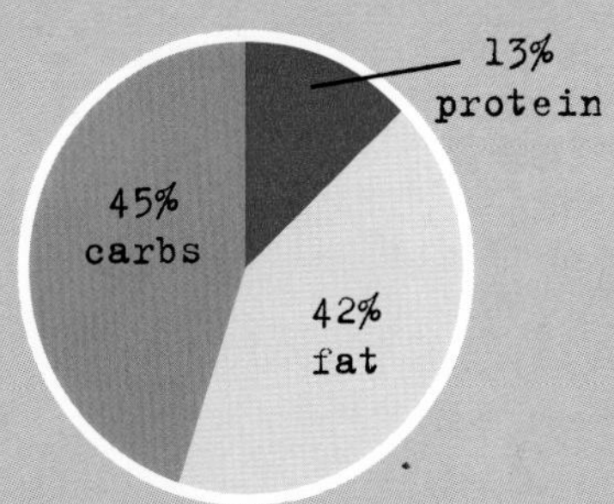

Carrots and Garlic

(3 servings)

5 carrots cut into thick match sticks
1 T olive oil
2 cloves garlic-chopped
1/4 c water
juice from 1 lemon

Heat oil over med high heat, add carrots and garlic and cook until the carrots start to turn golden brown while stirring occasionally. Add water and lemon juice and simmer until the carrots are tender about 4 minutes. Cook off the remaining liquid and salt and pepper to taste. Careful these guys will burn if you don't watch them.

Other Good Ideas!

-I serve these to guests with roasted chicken and they all love them

-Fantastic addition to Thanksgiving dinner!

This is a surprising sweet, savory and lemony side dish. Try it you'll love it.

Nutrition Per Serving

Calories - 90
Fat - 5g
Protein - 1g
Carbohydrates - 12g

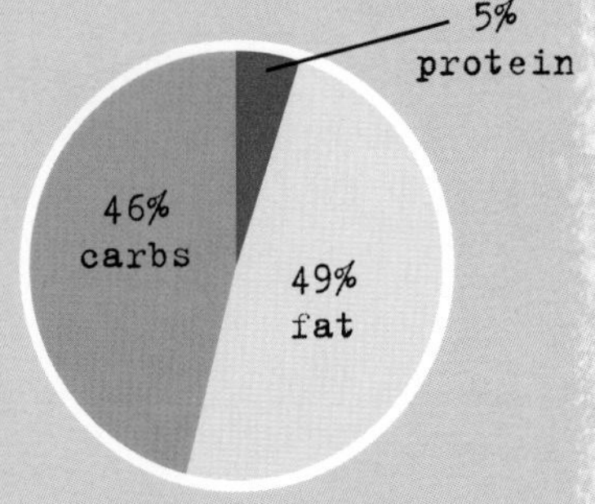

Roasted Broccoli

(3 servings)

1 large head broccoli with stems *-cut into 5-6 long pieces*
3 T olive oil
1 t garlic powder
3 T steak seasoning – the big chunky kind, any type

Preheat your oven to 425 degrees. Line a cookie sheet with foil or parchment if you want to reduce your cleanup. Put the oil and the seasonings into a large bowl. Toss in the broccoli and coat really well, especially the tops of the broccoli.

Remove the broccoli and place on the lined cookie sheet. Bake in the oven until the broccoli florets start to brown a little, about 10 - 20 minutes. The steak seasoning is just a coarse mix of pepper, garlic, and many other seasonings. There are many kinds of "steak seasonings" on the market right now but they are all good in this recipe.

Other Good Ideas!

–Make enough for leftovers as this is great in a salad too

–You can cook this on the grill with a holey grill pan or veggie cage

This recipe turned my husband into a broccoli lover.

I couldn't believe it when he actually asked me to make it.

It really changes the flavor of the broccoli.

Nutrition Per Serving

Calories - 80
Fat - 5g
Protein - 4g
Carbohydrates - 8g

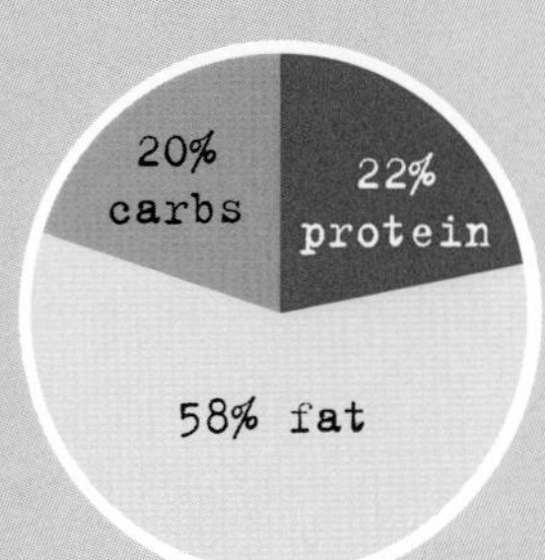

Roasted Balsamic Garlic Onions

These onions are worth the little extra effort.

They will add variety to your side dishes and salads as well as introduce new complex flavors to your favorite foods.

Nutrition Per Serving

Calories - 62

Fat - 5g

Protein - 1g

Carbohydrates - 5g

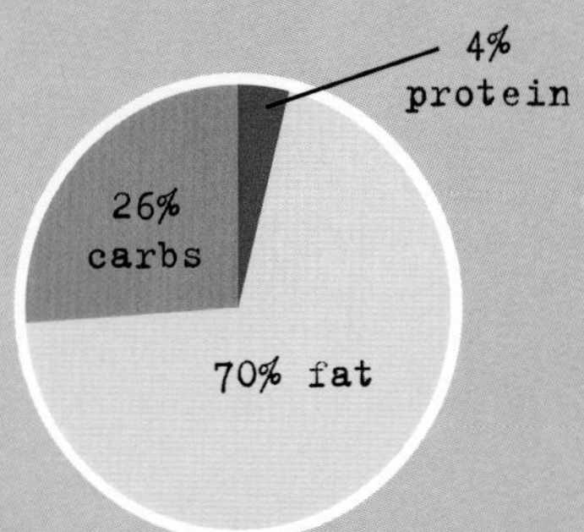

(3 servings)

1 large yellow onion sliced thickly
1 t olive oil
1 t balsamic vinegar
1 t garlic powder
salt

Preheat oven to 400 degrees. Spray cookie sheet with non stick spray or line sheet with foil to reduce cleanup. Mix all ingredients in a small bowl except salt and coat the onion slices really well. Cook for about 25 minutes then turn on the broiler if the onions aren't browned. Remove the onions and salt to taste. These are great served with most any meat but they are especially good on turkey burgers.

Other Good Ideas!

- –Chop up and put into your favorite chicken salad
- –Add to an onion dip
- –Add to a roasted salsa

Broccoli and Baby Bellas

(4 servings)

1 large head broccoli chopped into large chunks
1 small carton crimini mushrooms - *cleaned and trimmed*
4 T olive oil
1 T steak seasoning
4 dashes hot sauce
salt and pepper to taste

Preheat oven to 425 degrees.

Mix oil and seasonings into a large bowl then add veggies and toss well.

Spread veggies in a single layer on a cookie sheet. Cook for about 7-10 minutes. When the broccoli starts to brown on the tops it is done. Or you can stab a large piece of broccoli in the stem to see if it is cooked to your liking. I like it still crunchy with the tops lightly browned.

Other Good Ideas!

-Easy to do on the grill too

-Cool and chop to put into a salad with pecans and onions

Nutrition Per Serving

Calories - 68

Fat - 4g

Protein - 4g

Carbohydrates - 7g

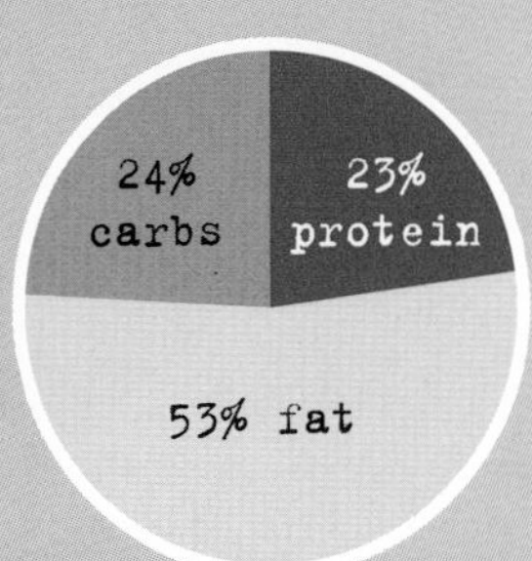

Shellie's Stuffed Mushrooms

by Shellie Collins

(4 servings)

1 carton of large sized button mushrooms *– wash and remove stems*

1/2 c low fat cottage cheese
2 slices bacon
1/4 c grated pepper jack cheese *(or use your favorite)*

Preheat oven to 350 degrees.

Wash and remove the mushroom stems. Place the stems in a food processor and chop until small bits. Now add the cottage cheese and the bacon into the food processor and chop until large sized chunks. Spray your baking sheet with non-stick olive oil spray. Stuff the mixture into the mushroom caps, sprinkle some of the cheese onto each mushroom cap and place into the oven for approximately 10-12 minutes.

You just gotta love Mushrooms!

Nutrition Per Serving

Calories - 78
Fat - 4g
Protein - 7g
Carbohydrates - 3g

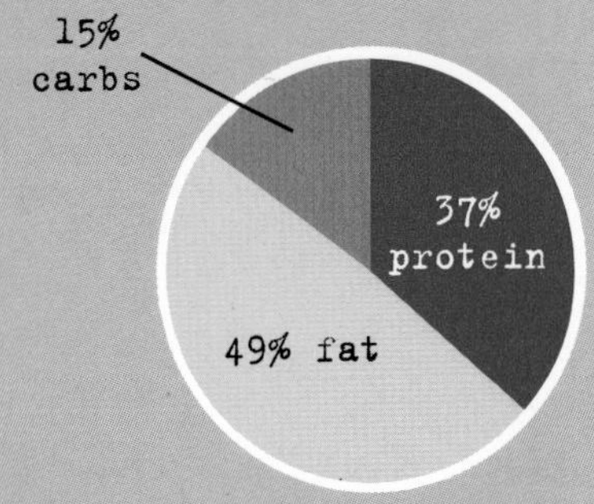

LEGUMES

Texas Style Pintos

(5 servings)

2 c dry pinto beans, rinse and check for rocks *(no kidding)*
10 or more shakes of hot sauce
1 t red pepper flakes
2 T crushed garlic
1 slice bacon
1/2 of a large onion-chopped
2 t garlic powder
1 T onion powder
1 bay leaf
1 t marjoram
1 t basil
1 1/2 t salt
lots of black pepper to taste

Soak dry beans for 12-24 hours then drain and rinse beans.

In a slow cooker, cover the beans with water or broth plus another 1 1/2 inches above beans. To the beans add the rest of the ingredients. Cook all day on low until the beans are very tender and the liquid has reduced to the top of the beans. Cooking times will vary on the freshness of the beans and the altitude of your kitchen. If you are cooking on your stovetop, bring the beans to a boil then reduce heat to low and simmer until the beans are tender.

Serve over 1/2 c of cooked brown rice. Garnish with diced sweet onion on top, diced jalapeno and some turkey ham if you want more protein.

This is how Grandma made her pintos for Sunday Supper.

Of course she made them with more bacon. But you don't need the added fat to have great flavor.

Nutrition Per Serving

beans served over 1/2 cup brown rice

Calories - 306

Fat - 2g

Protein - 14g

Carbohydrates - 59g

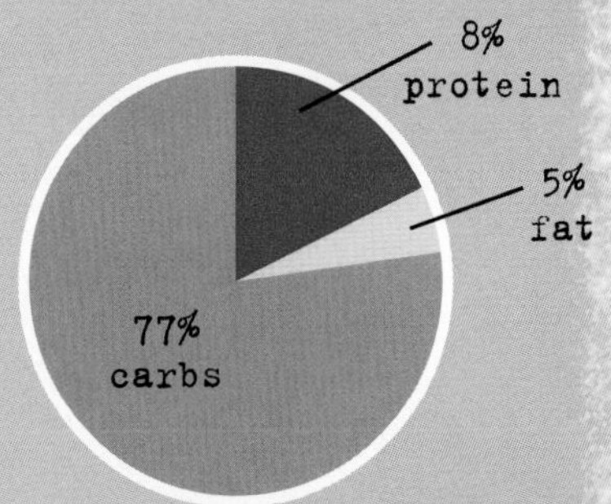

Other Good Ideas!

- Add pureed beans to soups and stews to make creamier
- Make "refried" beans or bean dip for parties. *(p.113)*
- Just use beans for your carbohydrate, as is
- Add beans to a cold salad
- If you are bothered by the 'gas' in the beans, try soaking them for a full 24 hours before cooking. It helps. Really.

Refried Texas Pintos

(3 servings)

3 c Texas Style Pintos (pg 112)
1/2 c salsa
salt to taste
pepper to taste
1/4 c diced onion
1 diced seeded jalapeno

Drain the beans in a colander for about 10 minutes but collect the liquid in a bowl. Do not rinse, just drain off most of the liquid.

Put the beans in a food processor and process till smooth or if you want it chunky, stop earlier. Add in the rest of the ingredients until just mixed. Serve hot or cold.

These make excellent refried beans when you heat them up and add a little shredded cheese to the top.

Other Good Ideas!

- –Spread on a tortilla with your eggs for a breakfast burrito
- –Make a layered party dip with guacamole and sour cream
- –Put on a pile of greens topped with chopped chicken
- –Use as a thickener for soups

Well these aren't really fried...

Now are they?

Nutrition Per Serving

Calories - 254
Fat - 1g
Protein - 15g
Carbohydrates - 48g

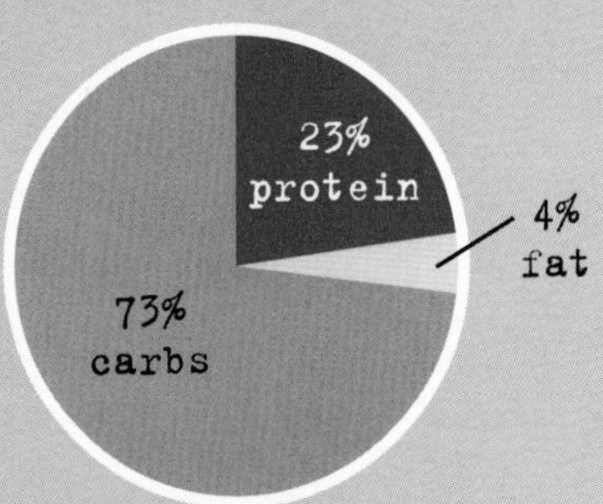

Creole Turtle Bean Salad

(3 servings)

1 can low sodium black beans - rinsed
1/2 c sliced of each of following
  mushrooms
  scallions or sweet onion
  celery
  yellow or red pepper

Dressing
2 T olive oil or flax oil
salt & pepper
1/8 t onion powder
1/2 t garlic powder
1/8 t hot sauce
1 t creole seasoning
2 T cider vinegar
1/8 t Old Bay seasoning

Mix everything together well and refrigerate. Before serving, mix in a serving size of tuna, chicken, or salmon.

Nutrition Per Serving

made with olive oil - no extra protein

Calories - 256

Fat - 10g

Protein - 11g

Carbohydrates - 32g

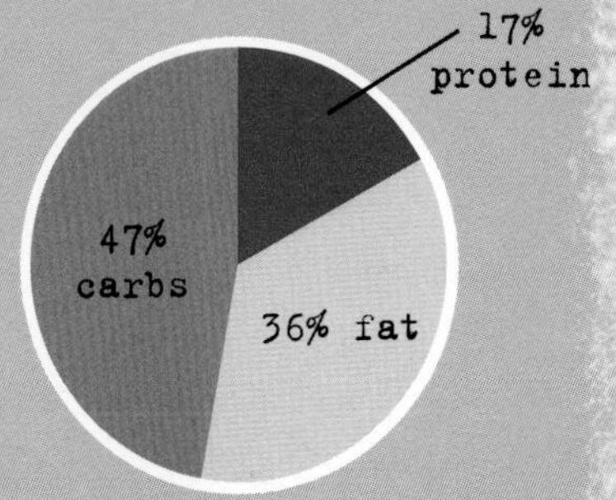

Other Good Ideas!

–Portable food- this works well in a travel container, just open and eat

–If you want less fat, use less oil and add more vinegar

Easy Butter Beans

(6 servings)

2 cans low sodium butter beans- rinsed
2 garlic cloves minced
salt and pepper to taste
1/8 t onion powder
1 c chicken broth
1/4 c salsa

Mix everything together in a med sauce pan. Bring to a boil then reduce to simmer for 15 minutes. Great side dish for chicken.

Other Good Ideas!

- Add to a salad
- Drain off liquid, puree the beans and use like you would refried beans or hummus.

Nutrition Per Serving

Calories - 218

Fat - 1g

Protein - 15g

Carbohydrates - 39g

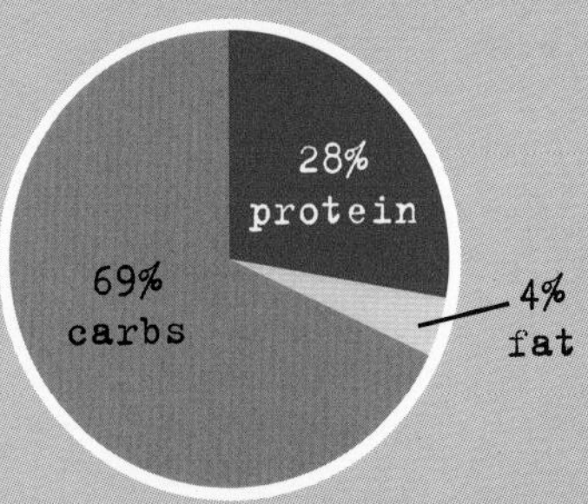

Cuban Black Beans & Rice

(6 servings)

1 T olive oil
1 large onion-chopped
1 large green bell pepper-chopped
5 large garlic cloves-chopped
2 t dried oregano
1 t cumin
3 bay leaves
2 15 ounce cans black beans-rinsed & drained
3/4 cup canned vegetable broth or water
1 T cider vinegar
1 c cooked brown rice

MMmmmmm beans.

Comfort food.

Heat olive oil in large saucepan over medium heat. Add onion, bell pepper, garlic and oregano and sauté until vegetables begin to soften, about 7 minutes. Add 1 cup of beans to pan. Using back of fork, mash beans coarsely. Add remaining beans, broth and vinegar and simmer until mixture thickens and flavors blend, stirring occasionally, about 15 minutes. Add 1 cup brown rice and mix together. Don't let the mixture dry out, if it does just add a 1/4 c of broth. Season beans to taste with salt and pepper and serve.

Other Good Ideas!

–This was created to serve with the Ropa Vieja (p. 49) but it works well with any roast beef or pork

–If you want this to have a kick, chop up a jalapeno and cook it with the vegetables

Nutrition Per Serving

Calories - 222

Fat - 3g

Protein - 11g

Carbohydrates - 38g

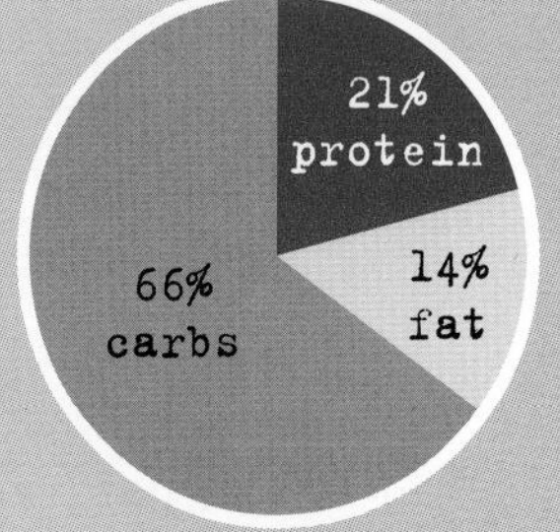

Baby Limas & Tomatoes

(4 servings)

16 oz frozen (pre-cooked) baby lima beans
2 slices turkey bacon - chopped
1/2 T olive oil
1/2 onion diced
1/2 t onion powder
1 t garlic powder
1 t curry powder
salt and pepper to taste
1/2 c chicken broth
1 can low salt diced tomatoes – drained
1 T dried or 3 T fresh parsley

Defrost the beans. In a large non-stick pan heat the oil on medium then add the chopped bacon. Let cook for 2 minutes then add the onion and cook for another 3 minutes until it starts to soften. Add the remainder of the ingredients and stir well. Simmer on medium low for 10 minutes or until the liquid starts to reduce and the beans are completely heated through.

Other Good Ideas!

–Refrigerate the beans and make a cold salad by adding some celery and chopped chicken

Very easy and fast side dish, just add chicken for a full meal.

Nutrition Per Serving

Calories - 155
Fat - 3g
Protein - 7g
Carbohydrates - 26g

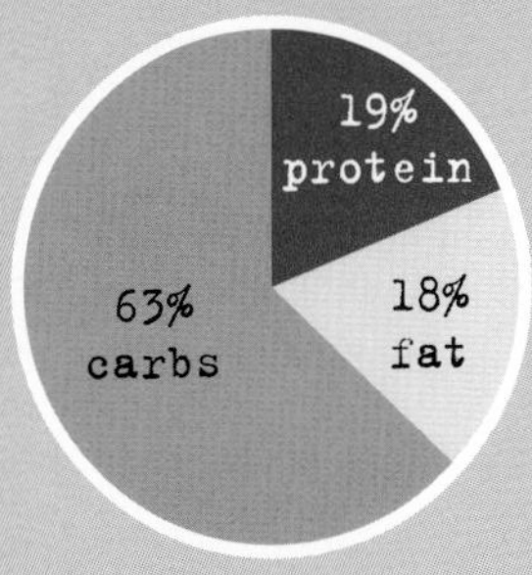

Easy Pinto & Tuna Salad

(4 servings)

3 c cooked pinto beans
12 oz tuna packed in water
5 scallions-chopped, bottom 5 inches
1 c chopped celery
3 T olive oil
1/2 T balsamic vinegar
1 T cider vinegar
5 shakes hot sauce
1 t coriander
1/2 t dry basil
1/2 t garlic powder
1 T lt. canola mayonnaise or your favorite
salt and pepper to taste

Mix everything together well. Refrigerate.

This is creamy, fresh and quick to create.

Other Good Ideas!

–Very portable

–Mix and match seasonings, very versatile

–Omit the mayo, it's still good

Nutrition Per Serving

Calories - 396
Fat - 14g
Protein - 31g
Carbohydrates - 36g

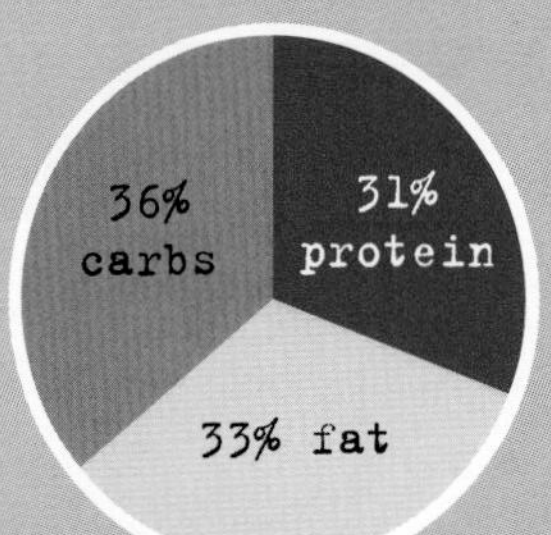

FRUIT & DESSERTS

Apple Crumble

(2 servings)

2 apples *(Braeburn, Fuji, or Granny Smith are all great)*
juice from 2 limes
2 T Succunat or honey *(succunat is a raw unprocessed sugar)*
2 T water
1/4 c old fashioned oats
1/4 t cinnamon
pinch salt
2 t cold butter

Use a pie plate sized dish for this.
Preheat oven to 375 degrees.

Peel, halve and core apples then slice thinly and put in bowl with lime juice and 1 T Succunat. Toss all together and then spread apples on bottom of dish. Sprinkle apples with the water. Bake for 20 minutes. Meanwhile…

While the apples are cooking, combine the remaining ingredients in a bowl and smush well with fingers or a fork trying to evenly distribute the butter.

When the apples are done, sprinkle with the topping and bake until the oats are golden, approximately 30 minutes.

Serve warm or room temperature.

THIS DESSERT IS SOOOOO GOOD. IT'S WARM, TART, CRUNCHY AND A LITTLE SWEET IN EACH BITE. YUM.

Nutrition Per Serving

Calories - 247
Fat - 7.5g
Protein - 3.5g
Carbohydrates - 44g

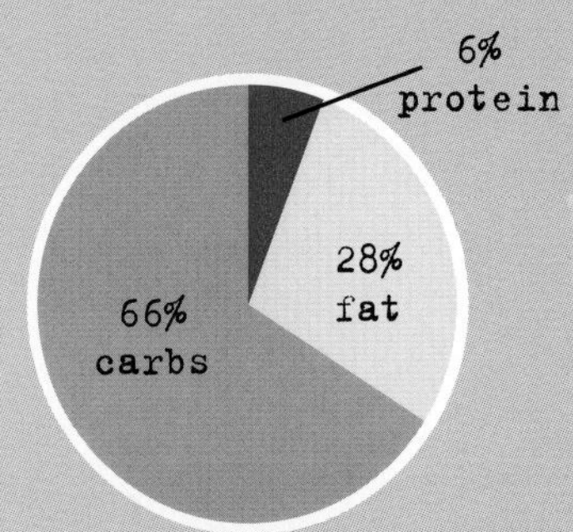

Other Good Ideas!

–Add dried cranberries or apricots to the apple mixture

–Top with a dollop of vanilla yogurt or ice cream

Pumpkin Cranberry Cookies

(24 Servings)

1/4 c softened butter
1/2 c Succunat *(Succunat is a raw unprocessed sugar)*
1/4 c unsweetened apple sauce
1/4 c honey
1 t vanilla extract
1 egg
1 c pureed pumpkin
1 c whole wheat flour
1/2 c oat flour *(you can make your own in a food processor or blender)*
2 t baking powder
1 t baking soda
1/2 t salt
1 t cinnamon
1 c cranberries-chopped
1 T orange zest
1/2 c pecans-chopped

Combine first 7 ingredients together and blend well. Combine all of the dry ingredients into a separate bowl and slowly add to the wet mixture until well mixed. Add in the cranberries, zest and nuts and mix by hand. Drop by rounded spoonfuls onto a greased cookie sheet and bake in a preheated oven at 375 degrees for 10-12 minutes. Makes 24 cookies.

Other Good Ideas!

- Add dried cherries or apricots to the mixture
- Add sunflower seeds or ground up flax seeds to really pack in more nutrition

These cookies are cake like and seriously tasty. My whole family devoured them over the holidays.

Nutrition Per Serving

Calories - 107
Fat - 4.5g
Protein - 2g
Carbohydrates - 17g

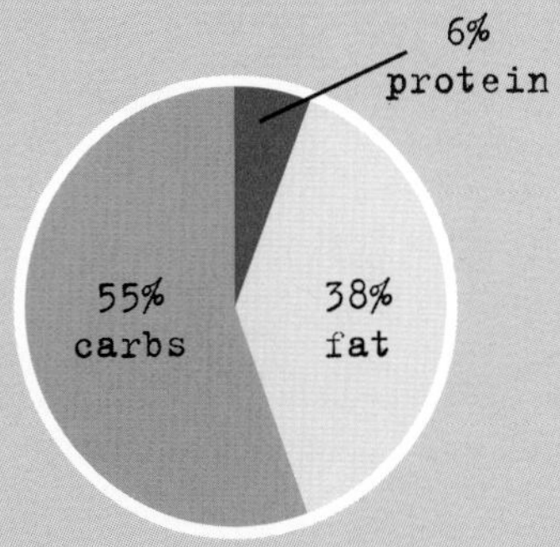

Amazing Apples

(3 servings)

3 cored apples *(Honeycrisp and Granny Smith are good choices)*
1/4 c chopped walnuts
1/4 c dried cranberries
2 T Succunat *(Succunat is a raw unprocessed sugar)*
1/2 t orange zest
1 c orange juice
1/4 c cranberry juice
1 T honey

In a small bowl combine nuts, cranberries, zest and Succunat. Stuff each cored apple with 1/3 of the mixture. Place the apples in a large slow cooker and drizzle the juice and then the honey over the tops of the apples. Cook all day on low or for a few hours on high or until tender.

Serve hot with some of the juice drizzled over the top and a dollop of vanilla yogurt.

Other Good Ideas!

–If you want to splurge, put a spoonful of vanilla ice cream on top before serving and let melt

The first time I made this I served it to a dinner guest. Let's just say he took one bite then all I heard was "yums, oohs & ahhs!".

Love it, especially since it's so easy.

Nutrition Per Serving

Calories - 322
Fat - 8g
Protein - 4g
Carbohydrates - 64g

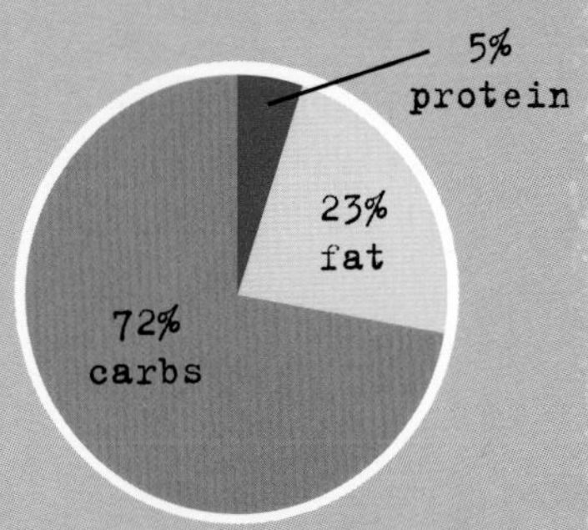

Fast Fruit Salad

(3 SERVINGS)

1 apple diced
1 banana sliced
1 orange chopped
small can chunk pineapple
1 small carton low fat pina colada yogurt
3 T chopped toasted pecans

Mix all together except the pecans just before serving and then top with the pecans. If you want to make this a little bit ahead, don't add the banana, yogurt or the pecans. Chop all of your fruit and mix and then add the juice of 1/2 lime or lemon to keep the apple from turning brown. Then right before serving, add everything else and top with the pecans.

A REALLY BASIC, YET SPECIAL WAY TO SERVE FRUIT.

Other Good Ideas!

–Use your favorite fruit

–Add dried fruit and toasted coconut for an ambrosia type salad

Nutrition Per Serving

Calories - 263

Fat - 7g

Protein - 5g

Carbohydrates - 48g

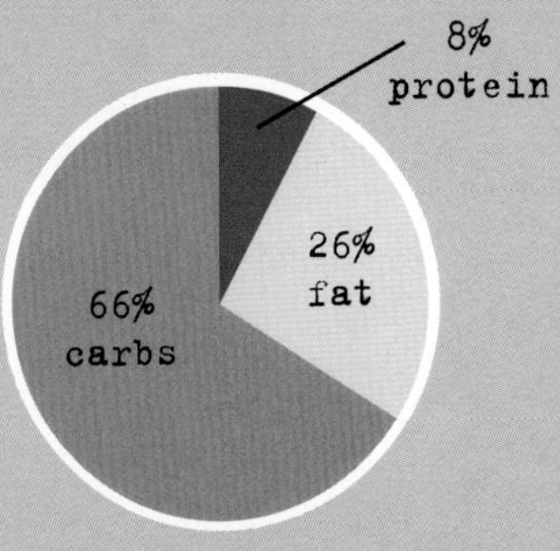

Quick Peanut Butter Cookies

(12 servings)

1 c natural peanut butter or any other
nut butter you like
1/2 c Succunat or 10 packets sweetener or stevia to taste *(Succunat is a raw unprocessed sugar)*
1/2 c oat flour
1 egg
1 t vanilla

Tender, peanut butter heaven.

Preheat oven to 350 degrees.

Make your oat flour in the blender or food processor. Dump into a medium bowl and add remaining ingredients. Mix well. Form 12 round cookies and press them partly flat onto a greased cookie sheet. Cook for approximately 20 minutes or until the edges are slightly brown. Remove carefully from cookie sheet, these are very tender. Let cool.

Other Good Ideas!

–Serve with a big glass of milk
–Try not to eat them all in one sitting

Nutrition Per Serving

Calories - 189
Fat - 12g
Protein - 7g
Carbohydrates - 16g

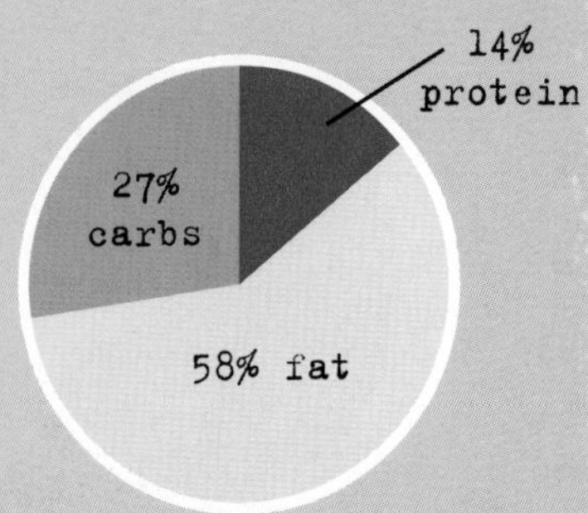

Dirt Balls

(14 servings)

1/ 4 c toasted old fashioned oats
2 T dry roasted sunflower seeds chopped
1/ 2 c natural peanut butter
2 T unsweetened cocoa
1/ 4 c chopped bittersweet chocolate
1 t vanilla extract
2 T roasted almonds chopped fine
1 small packet Stevia powder or 3 T honey

Toast oats in skillet on medium heat for about 20 minutes. While that's happening, combine the rest of the ingredients except for the almonds. Mix really well, a really strong fork works well. When the oats are finished toasting, chop them a little, in a food processor. Put into the mix and combine well.

Put almonds in a small bowl for rolling onto the balls.

If your mix is too sticky to handle, set in the fridge for 30 minutes or so. Make small balls about 3/4 of an inch across, roll in your hands then roll in the almonds. Voila-- nummies. Store in fridge in an airtight container.

Other Good Ideas!

-Add in dried cherries, coconut, puffed rice cereal, crushed bran flakes and lots of other goodies
–Roll in cocoa powder or powderd sugar

These little gems are a wonderful treat. My family loves them. They are also really good holiday gifts.

Nutrition Per Serving

Calories - 92
Fat - 7g
Protein - 3g
Carbohydrates - 6.5g

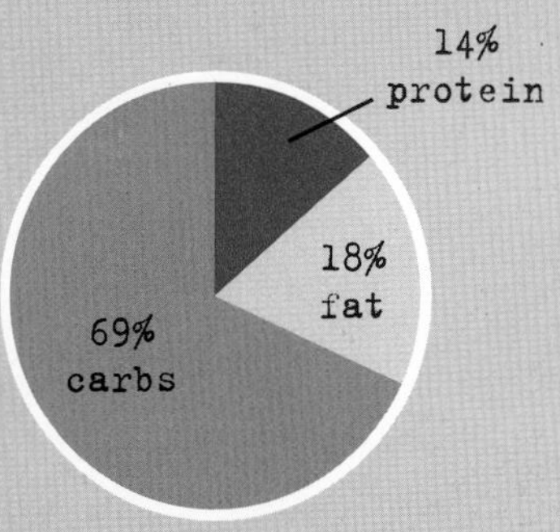

Frozen Peachy Dessert

(2 servings)

1 ripe peach – sliced
1/ 2 c low fat cottage cheese
10 drops Stevia liquid sweetener or small packet of favorite sweetener
1/ 4 t vanilla extract
1/ 2 c plain low fat yogurt

Low calorie summery fresh treat.

Blend everything together really well with a stick blender or a food processor until the cottage cheese is smooth. Please note you may need more sweetener depending on your tastes and your cottage cheese. Pour into a freezer proof container and place covered into the freezer for 30 minutes. Remove from freezer and stir well. Repeat the freezing process until you get the consistency you like. After 1 hour of freezing the dessert is almost the consistency of pudding. Freeze solid or eat after an hour.

Serve Topped with a dollop of vanilla flavored yogurt or some lightly sweet whipped cream.

Other Good Ideas!

-Try 2 cups of fresh or frozen strawberries as your fruit
-Mix in a serving of vanilla protein powder for more of a meal

Nutrition Per Serving

Calories - 97
Fat - 1g
Protein - 11g
Carbohydrates - 12g

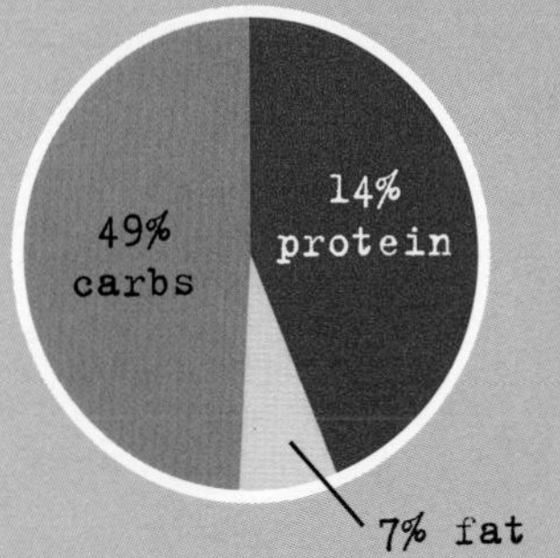

A Sweet, Clean Dessert

by Bradley Compton

(1 serving)

1 /2 c fat free cottage cheese
1 /2 c low sugar vanilla yogurt
2 T ground flax seed
dash cinnamon
2 apples cubed
3-4 fresh strawberries

Just mix well and eat. How easy is that?

A True Squeaky Treat!

Nutrition Per Serving

Calories - 386
Fat - 9g
Protein - 26g
Carbohydrates - 57g

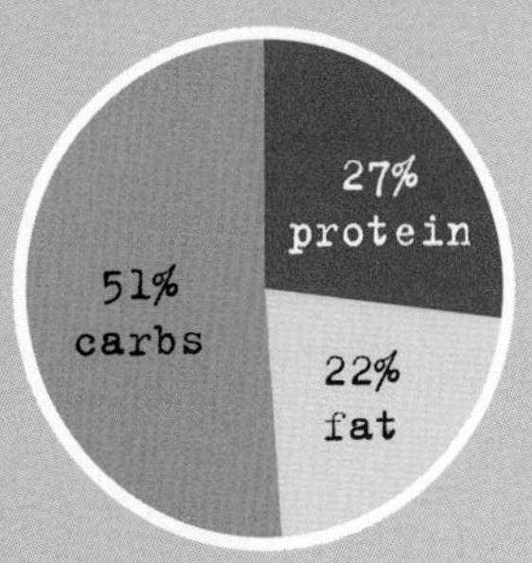

NOTES:

AVOCADO, DRESSINGS DIPS & NUTS

Easy Guacamole

(4 servings)

1 ripe avocado – mashed
1 lime – juiced
1/4 t garlic powder
2 T salsa *(use your favorite)*
2 T minced onion
salt & pepper to taste

Other Good Ideas!

–Smear this on your favorite burger or steak

–Party food

–Great for chili topper

Nutrition Per Serving

Calories - 138

Fat - 1g

Protein - 16g

Carbohydrates - 14g

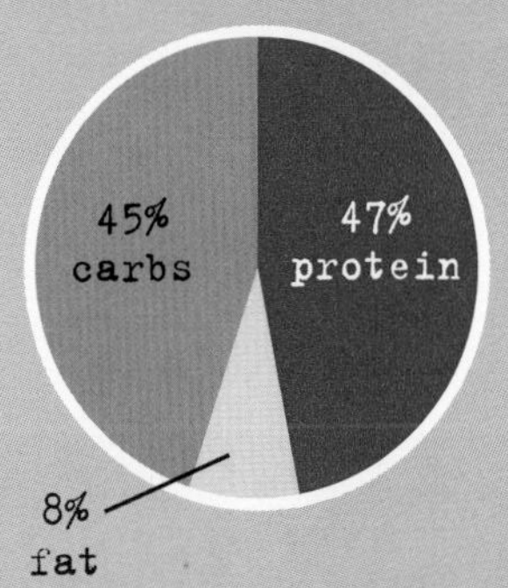

Cool Avocado Dip

(6 servings)

1 ripe avocado
1 8 oz container low fat plain yogurt
2 t cumin
1 t garlic powder
1/2 t salt
1/2 t hot sauce or more to taste

Put all ingredients into a food processor or blender and mix well.

Serve with your favorite vegetables or chicken wings for dipping.

Cool, creamy and green goodness.

Other Good Ideas!

- –Veggie Dip
- –Spread for turkey and grilled onion sandwich
- –Salad Dressing – just add a little cider vinegar to thin it out

Nutrition Per Serving

Calories - 83
Fat - 6g
Protein - 3g
Carbohydrates - 5g

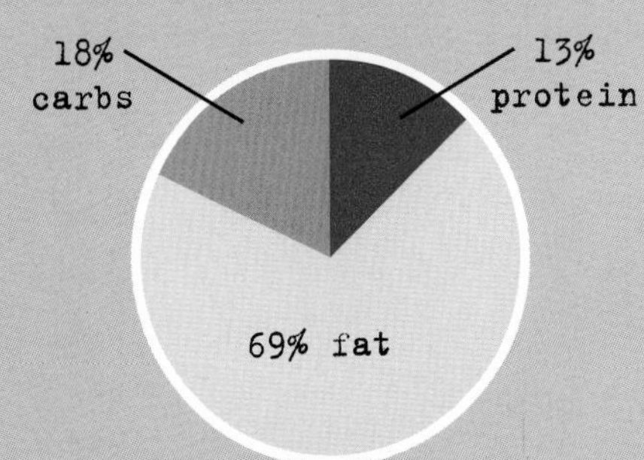

Fresh Avocado with Cumin

(4 servings)

1 ripe avocado diced
juice from 1/2 lime
salt and pepper to taste
1/8 t cumin
2 scallions diced *–whites only*

Mix ingredients well.

Other Good Ideas!

–Serve as a side dish with grilled steak or chicken or top your favorite salad with this easy dish.

–You can even add more veggies such as sweet red pepper and corn to make a more traditional salad

Nutrition Per Serving

Calories - 46

Fat - 5g

Protein - 1g

Carbohydrates - 2g

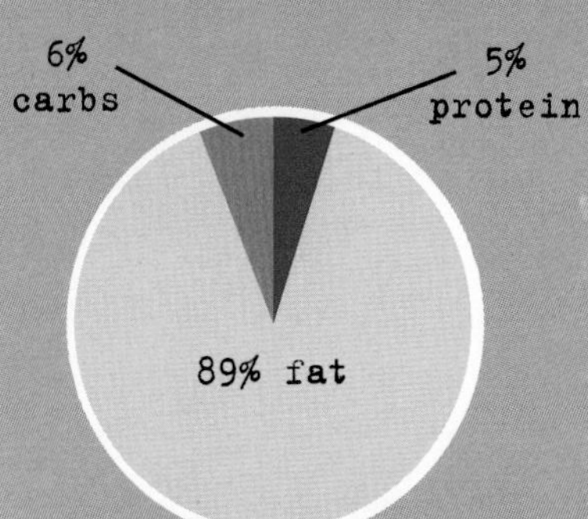

Green Chili Chipotle Dip

(5 SERVINGS)

1 pound low fat cottage cheese *–blended smooth*
5 T roasted garlic salsa
1 T chipotle chilis in adobo sauce *(canned)*
1 t cumin
1 t garlic powder
8 ounces non fat sour cream
1 t onion powder

Put all of the ingredients in a food processor or blender and blend until smooth.

Other Good Ideas!

–Great veggie dip or salad dressing

–This is also a great dressing for shrimp or beef tacos

Nutrition Per Serving

Calories - 105

Fat - 1g

Protein - 13g

Carbohydrates - 11g

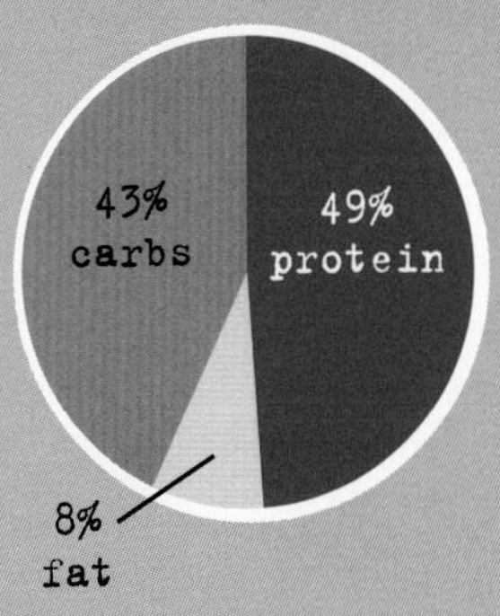

Killer Pecans

(6 servings)

2 c pecans, halves or pieces
1/4 c coffee liqueur
2 T chili powder
1/2 T canola oil or safflower oil
2 T granulated sugar
2 pinches salt
1/4 t cayenne pepper

Combine all ingredients together in a bowl except pecans and stir until all ingredients are mixed together. Add the nuts and mix until coated with the mixture. Spread in a thin layer on a foil covered baking sheet. Bake at 300 degrees for approximately 25 minutes stirring often. Separate the nuts from the foil and let cool.

Warning!
You can't eat just one.

Other Good Ideas!

-Party food you can even give as a gift
-GREAT for a late night snack
-Chop the nuts and sprinkle on your salads

Nutrition Per Serving

Calories - 279
Fat - 25g
Protein - 3g
Carbohydrates - 11g

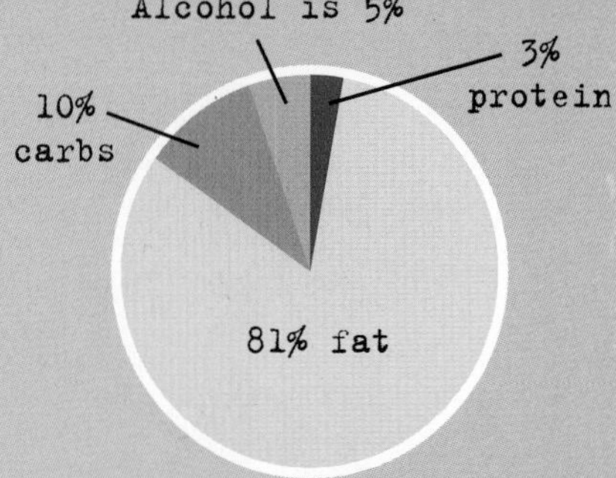

Balsamic Vinaigrette

(2 servings)

2 T olive oil
2 T balsamic vinegar
1/2 lemon juiced
salt & pepper to taste
1/2 t garlic powder

Combine all ingredients and blend or whisk well.

Other Good Ideas!

–This is great on all salads and grilled vegetables

–Good as a chicken marinade too

This is just a good basic salad dressing and marinade.

Nutrition Per Serving

Calories - 63
Fat - 7g
Protein - 0g
Carbohydrates - 0g

100% fat

Lemon Mustard Vinaigrette

(2 SERVINGS)

3 T apple cider vinegar
1 t onion powder
1 t garlic powder
1 t dill
1 t basil
2 T olive oil
1 T lemon juice
1 T Dijon mustard

Combine all ingredients and blend or whisk well.

Other Good Ideas!

–Another good chicken marinade

–Wonderful on a spinach salad topped with some toasted pecans

Nutrition
Per Serving

Calories - 67

Fat - 7g

Protein - 0g

Carbohydrates - 0g

100% fat

Yogurt Lime Dressing

(1 serving)

4 T plain yogurt
2 t fresh lime juice
1.5 t honey

Mix together really well. Serve over your favorite fruit salad.

Other Good Ideas!

–This is also a good chicken marinade, just add some garlic and fresh ginger

Nutrition Per Serving

Calories - 64

Fat - 0g

Protein - 3g

Carbohydrates - 13g

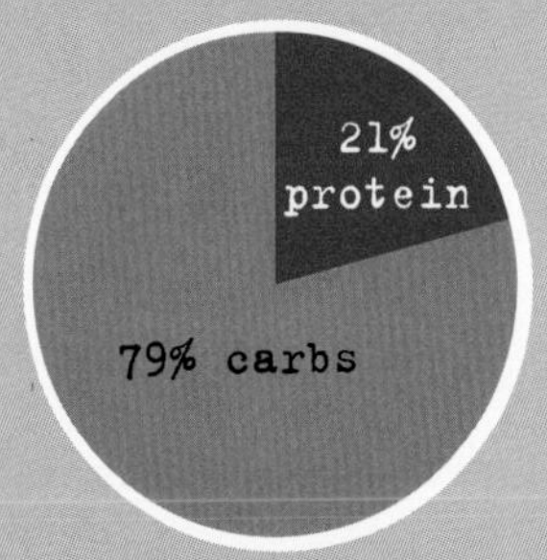

Toasted Spiced Pecans

(10 servings)

2 c pecan halves
1 t olive oil
2 t honey
1 T water
dash cayenne pepper
dash garlic powder
1 /4 t black pepper
1 /2 t sea salt

Heat skillet to med heat then add oil and pecans. Toast pecans for 10 minutes until they start to become a deeper brown. Stir often so they won't burn. In a small microwave proof bowl add the honey and water and heat a few seconds to melt the honey. Stir the honey water together well. Add the honey water to the pan and quickly stir to evenly coat all of the pecan halves. Stir often. Add the seasonings while the pecans are still wet. Stir occasionally so the honey doesn't burn. Keep cooking the nuts for another 10 minutes until they look dry.

Cool before serving.

Other Good Ideas!

-Walnuts work really well too

-Skip the garlic and add cinnamon and ginger for something different

-Use on top of your favorite salad

Nutrition Per Serving

Calories - 152

Fat - 15g

Protein - 2g

Carbohydrates - 5g

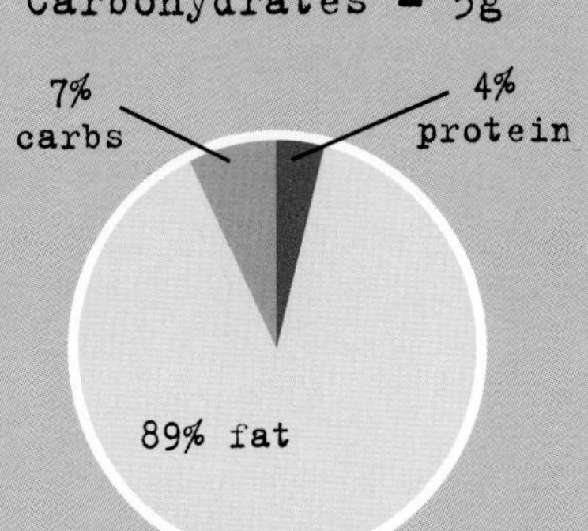

INDEX

R

S

T

V

W

Z

NOTES:

Notes:

Dedication:

" I would like to thank my family for standing by me as I journeyed down this road to fitness. Each of you stood by me and tolerated all the crazy notions and ideas I entertained. I want to thank my boys, Tony and Sebastian, for working out with me when I asked you to. I want to say a special thanks to my wonderful husband, Gregg, for always finding me beautiful no matter what shape or size I am. I love you all very much."
- Moe

" I want to thank my dear husband for helping with the book and honestly tasting everything I put in front of him, and to my daughter Kai for helping me remember why this is so important."
- Jamie

We want to extend A Special THANK YOU

(to Our Valued Friends and contributors)

John Birbari__________________________For his detailed eye in editing this project.

Rumaldo Hoglin__________________________For his sharp and artful skill of food photography.

Jason Wilson__________________________For his simple and clean design & layout skills.

Diet Power__________________________Nutritional calcualtions

THANK YOU AND PLEASE KEEP
FLAVOR ALIVE WHILE
LIVING WELL AND
EATING SQUEAKY
CLEAN.